Revolutionary Socialism by Louis Fraina
First Prism Key Press Edition 2011

Prism Key Press
New York, NY 10001
PrismKeyPress.com

ISBN-13: 978-1467902328

Revolutionary Socialism

A Study in Socialist Reconstruction
(1918)

Louis C. Fraina

Contents

Foreword

BOURGEOIS revolutions, like those of the eighteenth century, rush onward rapidly from success to success, their stage effects outbid one another, men and things seem to be set in flaming brilliants, ecstasy is the prevailing spirit; but they are short lived, they reach their climax speedily, then society relapses into a long fit of nervous reaction before it learns how to appropriate the fruits of its period of feverish excitement. Proletarian revolutions, on the contrary, such as those of the nineteenth century, criticize themselves constantly; constantly interrupt themselves in their own course; come back to what seems to have been accomplished, in order to start anew; scorn with cruel thoroughness the half measures, weaknesses and meannesses of their first attempts; seem to throw down their adversary only in order to enable him to draw fresh strength from the earth, and again to rise up against them in more gigantic stature; constantly recoil in fear before the undefined monster magnitude of their own objects until finally that situation is created which renders all retreat impossible, and the conditions themselves cry out: *"Hic Rhodus, hic salta!"* – Karl Marx, **The Eighteenth Brumaire of Louis Bonaparte**.

Preface

WARS, says Marx, are the locomotives of history. The world war is acting as an accelerator of events and as a drastic revealer of purposes and capacity. War cleanses and re-creates as it dirties and destroys. In the lightning-riven gulfs of the great catastrophe, Capitalism and the dominant moderate Socialism are each appearing in their true character and proportions, each proven unfit to direct the destiny of the world.

The world war signalized the collapse of the dominant Socialism; but it also signalized the advent of the proletarian revolution in Russia, organized and directed by revolutionary Socialism. Having cast off the petty bourgeois fetters that hampered its action, Socialism appeared as the revolutionary force and maker of a new world that are its essential characteristics. Out of defeats Socialism and the proletariat emerge with new vigor and vision.

The proletarian revolution in Russia marks the entry of the proletariat into a new revolutionary epoch. In this epoch the Social Revolution is no longer simply an aspiration, but a dynamic process of immediate revolutionary struggles. This is an historic development of decisive importance. It means the preparation of the proletariat for the final struggle against Capitalism and the necessity of an uncompromising policy in the activity of Socialism; it means, in short, the revolutionary reconstruction of Socialist policy and tactics, in accord with the imperative requirements of the new epoch.

The collapse of the dominant moderate Socialism was not a collapse of fundamental Socialism; it was a collapse simply of the contemporary historical expression of Socialism, and Socialism itself provides all the materials for the criticism of this collapse and for the reconstruction of Socialism.

The great task of Socialist reconstruction is proceeding actively throughout the world. It is a task that will require the co-operation of all the revolutionary elements of international Socialism. The complexity of forces and problems, the diversity of development, make co-operation mandatory. The old concepts of revolutionary Socialism will clash with the new, and the new with the old, until a synthesis emerges through the process of action and reconstruction. And the process of reconstruction will be animated by the struggles of the proletariat, not by the academic formulation of theory upon theory: Socialism is dynamic and not academic. Theory becomes an instrument of life, and not life an instrument of theory.

This book is a contribution to the task of reconstruction; its chief purpose is to provide a suggestive synthesis of Socialist reconstruction, and not an exhaustive analysis of all the problems involved.

I wish to express the deep appreciation I feel to my good Comrade, S.J. Rutgers, my colleague for one year on **The New International**, who read the manuscript of this book, making many an acute criticism and suggestion. A member of the revolutionary Social Democratic Party of Holland, Comrade Rutgers' sojourn of two years in this country and his activity in the Socialist Propaganda League were a source of inspiration and ideas to the comrades associated with him.

Louis C. FRAINA
New York City, November 6, 1918
First Anniversary of the Proletarian Revolution in Russia

Chapter I
Socialism and the War

WAR, particularly a general world war, tests the capacity of all whom it affects. The world war is a war that has thrown into the crucible of change all ideas and institutions; and out of this molten mass is emerging a new order.

This epochal character of the war is appreciated much more by the representatives of capital than by the representatives of the proletariat. Imperialism recognizes that all it cherishes is at stake; it recognizes that its future depends upon its action in this war, and its capacity to adapt itself to the new conditions that are developing. The old slogans, the old policy of Capitalism are being adapted to circumstances as they arise; it is inflexible in its class attitude during the war, and flexible in its attitude toward new problems, studying these problems, realizing that new conditions impose new measures. There is a ferment of ideas, a passionate activity, among the representatives of Imperialism, who appreciate the universal scope of the problems of the war. But, unfortunately, this attitude does not generally prevail among the representatives of the proletariat. Socialism itself is not in tune with the new rhythm of things. Socialism, on the whole, has during the war abandoned its class attitude. Socialism has met a real and humiliating defeat; and instead of recognizing this defeat as a defeat, in the spirit of men and of rebels, the tendency is either to explain away the defeat or hail it as a great victory. Instead of an appreciation of new conditions and new problems, the dominant Socialism smugly adheres to its old slogans and policy, the old tactics that directed Socialism straight to disaster. The great problems of a new epoch are compressed in the petty formulæ of yesteryear, – perverted formulæ, formulæ that have become a corpse which exhales the poisonous stench of death. This attitude is particularly apparent, largely dominant, in American Socialism; the war is used for purposes of petty

11

political advantages, and there is no appreciation, no attempt to appreciate, the revolutionizing importance of the war in its relation to Socialism.

The world war *is* a revolutionary factor. The war is transforming the world economically, socially and politically. Its importance has a dual character its influence on immediate events, and the ultimate changes and reconstruction it imposes upon the Socialist program and Socialist action. This process of transformation preceded the war and will continue after peace is concluded, the significance of the war being the circumstance that it has brought these preceding factors of transformation to a climax and powerfully accelerated their onward development.

The war marks the definite, catastrophic end of an epoch of Capitalism. It is not the end of Capitalism, as the *petit bourgeois* Socialist fondly imagines, – the *petit bourgeois* Socialist, who sees the end of Capitalism in any and all things except the dynamic struggles of Socialism and the proletariat. The old competitive Capitalism, the Capitalism of *laissez-faire*, of democracy and liberal ideas, has emerged definitely into a new epoch, the epoch of Imperialism. This transformation carries with it the alteration of old values and institutions, – an alteration being accomplished by Capitalism, but not, as yet, by Socialism.

Precisely as the nations at war are not battling for the mere division of territory or particular advantages, but for *general power,* so the transformation being wrought by the war is not measured in particular facts or institutional changes, but in the *general line of development* of Capitalism, and of the revolutionary proletariat: a new epoch, and a new alignment in the social struggle.

War develops out of the class struggle, and the class struggle develops in and through war. While bringing with it the collapse of Socialism as an organized movement, the war has simultaneously demonstrated, in a new way and emphatically, that the proletariat holds the future of the world in the hollow of its hand. Class antagonisms have been sharpened, while officially and apparently they have been modified through national unity; and Capitalism has shown its utter incapacity to preserve and promote civilization and progress. Moreover, the Russian Revolution has projected upon the stage of history the new revolutionary class *in action*, the class of the revolutionary proletariat. The Socialist conception of the proletariat as a class that will engage in the revolutionary struggle against Capitalism, and overthrow Capitalism, is no longer simply a theory, but a fact. Capitalism is a-tremble with apprehension at the accomplished fact of a proletarian revolution, and the danger that lurks in the awakening consciousness of the international proletariat.

Other factors than the Russian Revolution indicate the potential supremacy of the proletariat. The discussions of the war's military strategy emphasize the fact that the life of a nation, including its military power, lies in the workshops. The mobilization of the strictly military forces depends upon the mobilization of industry and the whole civil population. The: greater the industrial power of a nation, the greater its military power. Nor does the strength of a nation consist of its wealth, but of its *productive capacity*, – which means in the industrial proletariat. H.L. Gantt, an efficiency expert and shrewd observer of things industrial, says: "Soon after the breaking out of the war it was recognized that the life of a nation was to depend not upon the wealth it had stored up, but upon its productive capacity." Which is to say that wealth is simply a symbol, productive capacity the fact dominating all other facts. The war would have been over in short order if it depended upon the accumulated wealth of the belligerents; but it does not: it depends ultimately and in an economic sense upon the productive capacity of a nation, upon its industrial resources and the proletariat. Even a purely financial transaction such as a loan is not a transaction in wealth, but is based upon a nation's productivity, – a lien upon the future labor of the workers. The proletariat is dominant, economically; all the wealth in the world would shrivel into nothing, and Capitalism collapse, should the proletariat use its economic dominance in its own class interests and against the ruling class.

But while the war has proven the supremacy of the proletariat, and its latent revolutionary energy, the representatives of the proletariat during the war have been seduced by Imperialism. They have acquiesced in reaction, they have acted against the proletarian class.

One of the most interesting and significant events of the war is the mobilizing of labor and Socialism consciously into the service of Imperialism. Governments have calculatingly and as a policy used labor and "Socialism" in their activity, used them to inculcate in the workers the ideology of "carry on!" is, in a measure, indicates the power of the proleletariat; but it equally indicates that the dominant unionism and Socialism are betrayers of proletarian interests.

This government mobilization of the dominant unionism and Socialism against the revolutionary proletariat was a decisive development of the war. In the oncoming reconstruction of Socialism, this development will be a determining factor. All through the war dominant Socialism acted against fundamental Socialism, betrayed the proletariat, entered the service of Imperialism. The proletarian revolution in Russia had to dispose of its own moderate Socialism before it could dispose of the bourgeoisie; and after the proletarian revolution became an accomplished fact, the counter-revolution against the Soviet Republic was organized and directed by moderate Socialism. But not alone in Russia : in all other nations, moderate Socialism acted directly and aggressively against the proletarian revolution in Russia; intrigued against the Soviet Republic and the Bolsheviki. The proletarian revolution in Russia was a victory not only against Capitalism, but against moderate Socialism, and moderate Socialism, appreciating its coming disastrous defeat, united with Imperialism against the Workmen's and Peasants' Republic, against the revolutionary proletariat. Its attitude toward revolutionary Russia is the final, inescapable indictment of the infamous attitude of moderate Socialism during the war. Prior to the Russian Revolution, moderate Socialism might have justified its betrayal of trust; after, its attitude constitutes an indictment overwhelming in its force, terrible in its spirit, and inescapable in its proof. Socialism has been definitely split; a new and irrevocable formulation is necessary of fundamental Socialism.

The defects and betrayals that have characterized the dominant Socialism during the war were equally existent before the war, if less apparent. *The International did not collapse during the war; it collapsed before the war*, the war simply registering and emphasizing the collapse.

There is no complete break between war and peace – each is the expression of fundamental economic and political forces. The war marks a new epoch in Capitalism only in this sense, that it is the sharp, definite, catastrophic expression of forces operating in society during peace, and that precipitated war. Through war these forces are becoming dominant forces, where previously they were latent or only in process of development. The assumption, accordingly, that war marks a complete break with the preceding era is without a shred of historic truth. In other words, to understand adequately the politics and economics of Capitalism during war, its development and tendencies in the peace era preceding must be borne in mind ; and to understand the conflict of policy in the Socialist movement during the war, we must appreciate the fact that it is a continuation and a catastrophic expression of an identical conflict before the war. The form may change, the fundamental issues in dispute are identical, sharpened and emphasized by events.

Socialist policy, whatever apparently startling changes it may show, is not at all a breaking with the immediate past; the break with the revolutionary purposes of Socialism was made years ago. Socialist policy during the war is a direct result of the policy of yesterday, and can be considered only in that light. Peace and war – they are fundamentally identical, and each requires the same general course of revolutionary Socialist action.

The really great changes produced by the war, as developments of a previous tendency at work in society, are economic and political, not military. Nor do these changes affect simply the temporary mobilization of labor, industry and government for purposes of war. Their scope is larger and more permanent. The changes are not simply technical, but social and political; they do not consist in temporary adjustments of institutions and power, but in a radical alteration of their character. Moreover, the social-economic relations of classes are being revolutionized, and consequently their economic and political power, including the means of expression of their class interests. Prior to the war this alteration was being accomplished; it is being completed by the pressure of the war.

The dominant fact in this war is Imperialism. Imperialism is the animating and unifying tendency of all events; and Imperialism is itself the cause and effect of the tremendous changes that are being wrought in the economic, social and political structure of Capitalism.

The facts of contemporary political development are incomprehensible unless related to Imperialism. And it is a mistake of the first importance to consider Imperialism simply in relation to war. The international aspects of Imperialism – the export of capital, the struggle for investment markets, raw materials and undeveloped territory, and war – are not alone important; the decisive factor is the alteration of class relations and class power that Imperialism produces in each particular nation. The internal and international aspects of Imperialism are one, develop and supplement each other. To consider Imperialism in its international aspect alone is to misunderstand its nature and to cripple our power of fighting effectively

16

against it and for Socialism.

Not the least vital feature of Imperialism is its influence on Socialism. If the social-economic and class relations of Capitalism are being altered by Imperialism, it means that Socialism must necessarily undergo a tactical transformation and reconstruction in order to adapt itself to the new conditions.

The war and Imperialism pose the problem: either Imperialism and war, or Socialism and the new order.

The war marks the violent efforts of Capitalism and Imperialism to break through the multiplying contradictions of a decaying class system. That is the general formulation of the problem. Specifically, and more important, the problem assumes this form: either the proletariat must repudiate moderate Socialism and accept revolutionary Socialism, or Imperialism will become impregnable, and drag the whole world through a new series of wars irresistibly on toward the collapse of all civilization.

Chapter II
Imperialism and Capitalism

I

Imperialism characterizes the new, the final stage of Capitalism. It characterizes, equally, the unity of all the forces of Capitalism into a new and more formidable instrument of conquest and spoliation, the final desperate maneuver of Capitalism to prevent its utter disintegration and collapse. [1] Imperialism, accordingly, is a fundamental manifestation of Capitalism, Capitalism at the climax of its development.

This fundamental character of Imperialism is the decisive factor in contemporary world-development. All forces and all tendencies, all aspirations of Capitalism, are being merged into the new imperialistic epoch, now definitely established as the dominant expression of Capitalism. This dominance is not a consequence of the war, but the war is a consequence of the dominance of Imperialism. As a major or minor factor, Imperialism controls the policy of states, and determines alignments in the social struggle. Economically and historically, the characteristics of Imperialism justify its designation as a new stage of Capitalism, not an accidental or transitory manifestation.

But this characterization of Imperialism is not generally accepted. Among the liberals, and among the liberal-"Socialists," Imperialism is considered a temporary product of Capitalism, that may be disposed of upon the basis of Capitalism. The government Socialists in all belligerent nations, who represent groups of the working class seduced by Imperialism, accept wholly the conception of modifying and ultimately disposing of the antagonisms of Imperialism upon the basis of Capitalism: their policy of social-reformism is a policy that depends upon Imperialism, is a phase of social-

Imperialism, and they wish to perpetuate the policy of social-Imperialism, while avoiding its horrors. Imperialism is conceived as being fundamentally alien to Capitalism, as the product of particular capitalist and militarist interests, and not an expression of unified Capitalism. This conception constitutes a total misconception of the historical character of Imperialism; it is, moreover, an expression of *petit bourgeois* Socialism, which, because of its policy of reformism, must adapt itself to Capitalism and avoid the revolutionary struggle. The characterization of Imperialism as a definite stage of Capitalism goes to the heart of contemporary problems, and of the revolutionary reconstruction of Socialism.

Imperialism is the contemporary expression of the requirements of dominant Capitalism. Industrial monopoly, finance-capital, the whole process of capitalist production *as an historical category*, all layers of the ruling class, the policy of social-reformism, are now dependent upon the adventures and conquests of Imperialism, financial, industrial, and military. The rapid development of Capitalism nationally has simultaneously limited its base internationally; the broadening of economic opportunity of one nation circumscribes the opportunity of a competing nation. While Capitalism is organized nationally and functions nationally, capitalist economy is becoming, is now dependent upon the facts of international production. Capitalism attempts to solve this contradiction through Imperialism, apparently successfully, but actually multiplying the contradictions of Capitalism. Competing Imperialism clashes with competing Imperialism; and the whole of Capitalism becomes absorbed in this clash, since the prosperity of a nation depends upon its Imperialism. Imperialism is the characteristic and unifying tendency of the final stage of Capitalism.

Out of competitive Capitalism develops monopolistic Capitalism; and out of monopolistic Capitalism develops Imperialism. The policy, the tendency, the ideologic-political forms of the imperialistic epoch differ in fundamentals from the epoch of competitive Capitalism. This alone characterizes

Imperialism as a definite stage of Capitalism. Moreover, as the final stage of Capitalism, Imperialism imposes a stern obligation upon Socialism – the obligation of Socialism adapting itself to the revolutionary requirements of the new epoch.

II

The economic power of motion in capitalistic society is the accumulation of capital through competition, and the development of monopoly through the accumulation of capital. This process is dependent upon the production of surplus value by the workers. Capital yields profits, which are invested and in turn become capital. The accumulation of capital accelerates industrial expansion, and this expansion reacts upon and accelerates the accumulation of capital and the development of monopoly.

Historically, Capitalism comes into being through the expropriation of the peasantry from the soil, (by the brutal and infamous means of fire and sword,) the creation of a large body of proletarians which become the human raw material of industry, and the industrial development of the internal market. For a definite period, the requirements of the home market are largely sufficient for the purposes of industrial expansion and accumulation. The principle of competition, of *laissez faire*, dominates the activity of Capitalism, as well as, largely, the relations of nations to each other. The development of the national economy absorbs the capital and the efforts of the *entrepreneur*; capital is permanently invested in means of production, in machinery, through which the internal market is developed and the nation becomes industrialized. Trade between nations consists of the export and import of consumable goods. But capital accumulates, and is invested in more means of production; and the point is finally reached where the home market, the strictly national economy [2], no

21

longer serves the purposes of industrial expansion, no longer absorbs the masses of investment capital, and the new means of production which become the permanent form of the investment of capital.

The accumulation of capital, in one sense, depends upon the existence of low wages, which in itself creates the contradictions inherent in the accumulation of capital and the capitalist economy. The prevailing low wages – the extraction of surplus value – implies the inability of a nation to consume all the products it produces. These surplus products are exported to other countries at a lower stage of industrial development; but thereupon these countries emerge definitely into the capitalist mode of production, become industrialized, and produce a mass of surplus products of their own.

"When the newcomer within the family of capitalist nations turns from a customer of its older capitalistic brethren into their competitor, it does not do so in all fields of production. On the contrary, it continues to remain their customer for a long time to come. Only it does not buy from them any more textiles and other consumable goods as it used to, but machinery and means of production generally. The competition of the newcomer in the production of consumable goods leads to a shifting of production in the older – industrially more developed – countries. These countries now produce, proportionately, more machinery and other artificial means of production and fewer consumable goods." [3]

This development proceeds upon the basis of the accumulation of capital, which accumulates at a terrific pace. But this creates a mass of surplus capital, which is not absorbed by the development of the internal economy, exactly as surplus products are not absorbed. An impetus is provided this development by the appearance of monopoly, which unifies the industrial process of a nation, and aspires after world monopoly. Monopolistic Capitalism, having monopolized the national economy, becomes international and tries to monopolize the investment markets and sources of raw material throughout the world. This again accelerates the accumulation of capital, the production of means of production, the necessity of developing new industrial markets to absorb the accumulating mass of surplus capital and means of production. [4] An *impasse* is reached – capitalist production must break its national bonds and become international; new spheres of economy must be secured for industrial development, to absorb surplus capital and means of production; new sources of raw material must be conquered and monopolized, a new capitalism must be "created" *and* monopolized by the older Capitalism in order to prevent its disintegration and collapse. It is a desperate situation, and Capitalism resorts to desperate means to avert impending collapse. The peaceful economic partition of the world proceeds feverishly; but each partition produces new appetites, and narrows the economic opportunity of competing capitalistic nations. Contradictions multiply, antagonisms assume a more impelling and irreconcilable character; and the ultimate arbitrament of the issues in dispute becomes the arbitrament of the bayonet. Capitalism emerges definitely into a new phase of its existence, – Imperialism: the climax of Capitalism, the final stage of its supremacy.

This new stage of Capitalism completely alters the colonial policy of the great industrial nations. Commercial colonialism was a factor of the utmost importance in the development of Capitalism. The wealth filched from the colonies becomes an accelerator of the accumulation of capital in the mother country, contributes to the development of the internal industrial technology. At first the process is simply one of stealing gold, silver, and other precious articles from the natives, who are exterminated; but this policy, persisted in, produces an industrial stagnation in the mother-country that brings about its ruin, as in Spain. The country is choked in its own ill-gotten wealth. It is only where this appropriation of wealth coincides with a normal development of industry, as in England, that it promotes Capitalism. This development produces an ever increasing mass of products, which are exported to the colonies. The ability of the natives to consume is artificially stimulated, and they are compelled to use products which their primitive minds do not desire, and at the same time they are put to work to produce those special articles required by the nation that rules them. The natives are "civilized" in order that they may yield profits.

But the older colonies are incompatible with the capitalist mode of production, which pre-supposes the expropriation of the laborer. Laborers exported to the colonies become independent and refuse to submit to the capitalist mode of production, preferring to till the soil which is abundant and secured without cost. The trade in goods of developing nations with each other constitutes a more efficient means of capitalist accumulation. Capitalism begins to consider colonies as unprofitable, and they are largely retained because of the bureaucracy of officials for whom they provide employment, and because of special opportunities for robbery given to a few members of the ruling caste. This period, however, passes away in the measure that the capitalist mode of production enters a new phase. The colonies establish an organized life; the import of products is supplemented by the import of capital, and the colonies become active producing units by the import of means of production. The colonies are now active industrial producers, absorbing surplus capital; and the mother-country now fights to retain these colonies.

It is precisely the nations with an old established colonial system, such as England, that first pass into the epoch of Imperialism; or a nation, such as the United States, that has at its doors an undeveloped territory which plays the part of a colony. The colonial system under Imperialism undergoes another change, and that is the practical cessation of immigration to these domains. The natives are no longer exterminated to make room for the whites, but are expropriated from the soil and turned into wage-laborers, become the human raw material of industry, historically the basis of the capitalist mode of production. The migration of men to the colonies is supplemented by the migration of capital, of means of production; occupied territory is not to be colonized, but "developed" and exploited. The "pressure of population," by which some explain the phenomenon of Imperialism, is a myth; Germany, which has been striving to carve out a colonial empire, has no desire to export its people, but to export its capital and machinery. France has been active in the struggle for territory, and France has no surplus population to export.

Imperialism does not concern itself with colonies alone. It extends its scope to countries which can in no sense be colonial possessions, but which because of an inferior stage of industrial development, provide opportunity for the investment of capital and the introduction of a modern industrial technology. Protectorates and "spheres of influence" become the new means of aggrandizing national capital; or if these are insufficient the country may be occupied, in order to assure stability and normal development. France did not occupy Morocco in order to colonize it, but to assure French investors security and a monopoly of the profits that come from developments. The great industrial nations transform their colonial possessions into producers and absorbers of surplus capital; and reach out to develop any other part of the world, civilized and uncivilized, in which the investment of capital will yield more than average profits. Not the least attractive feature of this policy for the capitalist is the existence of a mass of low-priced workers in an undeveloped territory – low wages being a particularly powerful accelerator of the accumulation of capital, other things being equal.

Having revolutionized industry within its own national borders, accordingly, Capitalism now revolutionizes industry within the borders of undeveloped nations, creates a new proletariat and a new Capitalism which become the base upon which are erected new systems of empires, financial and military. Hitherto, all that these undeveloped lands were required to do was to purchase the consumable products of the great industrial nations; but this is now insufficient, and Capitalism begins to develop and exploit the new markets through the investment of capital and the introduction of machinery. It becomes no longer sufficient, for example, that Mexico sell the United States its agricultural products and raw materials, and that it purchase the manufactured products of the United States. The Mexican home market must be developed; it must absorb the surplus capital of United States Capitalism, purchase its iron goods and means of production, which become dominantly the form of investment of accumulated capital. Then comes the period of the investment of American capital in Mexico, the building of railways, docks, and factories by American enterprise and American money. This is the export of capital, the animating factor in Imperialism. The domination and exploitation of undeveloped peoples becomes the characteristic of parasitic Capitalism. The climax of this development is a change in the economic policy of a nation, in the character of its politics. [5]

The great fact of international economics during the past thirty years is the investment of British, French, German and American capital in the undeveloped sections of the world, – China, Egypt, Mexico, Central and South America, Africa, the Balkans and Asia Minor; a process of investment which rapidly emerged into definite Imperialism.

But this purely economic fact goes hand in hand with a vital political fact the struggle for and extension of political control over these undeveloped lands by the nations exporting capital. These nations do not simply compete in the export of capital, but a fierce rivalry arises to secure political control in the countries where capital is invested, a control that constitutes the mechanism of monopolistic Capitalism. The reason for this is dual:

1. It does not matter so much to a capitalist whether a country has a stable government or not, as long as he is simply selling its people consumable products. Such a

country may be convulsed by revolutions, disorder may reign, but it matters little if only the products are paid for, and that is the end of the transaction. As soon, however, as the foreign capitalist invests money in the country, either as loans to the state or in "projects of development," its government and social order become of the utmost importance. Revolutions, and a pre-capitalistic social order generally, disorganize industry, and the invested capital yields no profits; may, moreover, become a dead loss. The export of capital and its investment immediately develops its ideology, – a horror of revolutions, the lamenting of disorders, a Crusader's enthusiasm for making over the country in the image of sacrosanct Capitalism, and the pious desire that the people should live in "peace" and "prosperity," under the domination of a "superior race" if necessary. The capitalist, accordingly, brings pressure to bear on his own government to maintain order in the country where his money is invested, and the government becomes guarantor of his investments. Imperialistic governments unblushingly and unashamed develop into agencies to collect debts and promote investments; the army and navy become adjuncts of the banks and of investment capital. It was the boast of imperial Rome that it protected its citizens wherever they might wander; it is the pride of imperialistic governments that the capital of their citizens is protected wherever it may be invested. These governments try to prevail upon a backward country to maintain order and the stability of industrial activity; this failing, a protectorate is established or the country bodily annexed. Peace and prosperity prevail – for the investor!

2. Finance capital, which is the factor behind Imperialism, is essentially monopolistic, the nerve center of monopolistic Capitalism. The investment markets of the world (and sources of raw material) are limited, and each national Capitalism seeks their control for itself and

the exclusion of others. The finance and politics of Imperialism are indissolubly linked, and the political control of a backward country is indispensable to the purposes of Imperialism. There ensues, accordingly, a struggle between national Capitalism not only for investment markets, but for their political control. This is the meaning of the Franco-German clash over Morocco; Anglo-German rivalry in Mesopotamia; the schemes of Japan for control in China; and the transformation of the Monroe Doctrine into an imperialistic instrument for establishing American capital in monopolistic control of Central and South America. [6] The financial and the political facts, moreover, are linked together by the circumstances that it is not simply investments, but the *development* of a country which is the ultimate and necessary object of Imperialism.

In the operations of Imperialism politics are inseparable from economics. The Bagdad Railway, by which German Imperialism sought to insure its control of the development and exploitation of Mesopotamia and Asia Minor, was as much a matter of politics, if not more so, as of finance; and it was this feature that produced the diplomatic clash between Germany and Great Britain, which prevented the railway being completed. Military conquest is a means of promoting Imperialism, and the operations of Imperialism, through control of territory, railways, etc., are calculated to promote ultimate conquest. Hence the political character of Imperialism and the antagonisms it develops between states. The loans that have from time to time been granted to China by the Great Powers have been political transactions in which finance, as an immediate factor and purpose, played a secondary role; the loans were used to secure political or territorial concessions from China; and it was through the medium of these political loans that national sovereignty largely passed out of the hands of China into the control of these other nations. Nor were these loans granted by finance alone, but by finance acting in co-operation with its particular national government. Finance promotes politics and politics promotes finance.

The export of capital to an undeveloped country, whether it assumes the form of loans to the Chinese government or the building of the Baghdad Railway, does not end with the particular immediate transaction. This immediate transaction, it is true, absorbs a certain amount of surplus capital; but it is secondary in importance to ultimate purposes, to the *subsequent* absorption of surplus capital. The Bagdad Railway constituted a means by which the whole region of Mesopotamia and Asia Minor was to be developed industrially, a development absorbing new surplus capital and products; it was to act much as the great transcontinental railway systems of the United States, – to open up new territory for industrial use and prepare the way for intensive development and exploitation. It was this subsequent development which was to justify the Bagdad Railway, the opening up of a new internal market, the development of a modern industrial technology in these capitalistically and wastes, and consequently the absorption of large masses of German capital and means of production. The political privileges wrung from China – usually "concessions" and "spheres of influence" – were claims upon the natural and industrial development and exploitation, which would require again the export of capital. It is this economic fact that produces the necessity of political control in an undeveloped country that is the objective of Imperialism.

Another animating cause of Imperialism, of minor or major importance according to the resources of a country, is the competition to secure raw materials, particularly iron, oil and coal. As a nation reaches the maturity of development of its internal market, it reaches the point where itst internal raw materials are either becoming exhausted or are insufficient for its industrial purposes. These raw materials must be secured abroad, in undeveloped countries. Iron is the basis of the modern industrial technology, the constituent element in the production of means of production, and oil is becoming a prime factor in transportation, since the invention of the Diesel engine. A supply of the raw materials necessary for industry, constant and uninterrupted, is a matter of life and death to Capitalism. In the earlier Colonial era, colonies were prized in the measure that they possessed silver and gold; in the iron age of imperialistic Capitalism, iron ore, copper and other industrial metals are of utmost necessity, and their possession may make a nation rich beyond the dreams of avarice. The development of mines in undeveloped countries performs a two-fold function – it absorbs surplus capital, and provides the mother-country with the raw material of industry, which is largely converted into means of production for export to undeveloped countries. China is simply bursting with iron ore and other metals, and Japan is hungry for their possession, as it has practically none within its own territory; the iron ore of Morocco [7] was the motive of the desire of Germany and France to secure control in that region; the inexhaustible oil wells of Mexico have for the past ten years been the source of a bitter struggle for their possession between American, British and German capital. Bismarck seized Alsace-Lorraine for political, territorial and dynastic purposes; but to-day Germany refuses to relinquish these provinces because, other reasons aside, they are rich in iron ore, having in 1913 produced 21,136,265 metric tons of iron ore as against 7,471,638 metric tons produced by the rest of Germany. This struggle for raw material, particularly iron ore, is, together with the export of capital, a distinguishing feature of Imperialism and a symptom of the fact that national Capitalism is now at the climax of its development.

Imperialism is a process of expropriation – the expropriation of a national Capitalism by its competitor. Imperialistic Capitalism may, by means of a particularly perfected monopoly, engage in competition against a rival Capitalism within its own nation, and expropriate it in *its own* markets. Moreover, Imperialism does not simply covet undeveloped territory, but may annex *developed* territory, providing it possesses raw materials and the capacity to absorb capital. Powerful industrial and financial interests in Germany urge the annexation of Northern France – the metallurgical and manufacturing centre of France; and the annexation of Belgium. The first would strike a terrific blow at French Capitalism; the second would expropriate a whole national Capitalism and aggrandize German Capitalism. Detaching Alsace-Lorraine from Germany, on the other hand, would mean economic disaster – unless Germany secured "compensation" by annexing the Baltic provinces of Russia, which are rich in raw materials. Monopoly – the monopoly of a particular national Capitalism – would be established in the conquered regions by means of the expropriation of nascent or dominant Capitalism; and, this monopoly organized, a new struggle would emerge for world monopoly and world power.

III

Monopolistic Capitalism and Imperialism are necessarily belligerent. As the expropriation of one capitalist by another was a means for the accumulation of capital, so the destruction of capital and the expropriation of a competing Capitalism through war becomes a means for the perpetuation of Capitalism. In this desperate way is Capitalism maneuvering to prevent a decrepit system from tottering to its collapse.

In the process of imperialistic competition, governments and their diplomacy and armed power become conscious and active agents in the promotion of the Imperialism of their particular capitalist class. In ways sinister and secret, open and unashamed, governments act as the panders of Imperialism, raping the peace of the world and the independence of peoples.

This competition in the export of capital is financial and political; and being political and promoted by governments, there arises a situation in which war becomes a perpetual menace. The ultimate economic fact develops an ideology and a justification, – the "white man's burden," the "defense of small nations," the concept of a "superior race" invested with the mission of imposing its "*kultur*" upon the backward races, the aspiration of "making the world safe for democracy," and the "defense of the nation and its institutions." The activity of diplomacy and a recourse to war are justified through these ideologic concepts; but, in fact, it is the economic process of the export of capital and the expansion of industry, jointly with the necessity of crushing rivals by armed force and securing control of the exploitation of the undeveloped regions of the world, that act as the driving force of imperialistic diplomacy and war.

Imperialism is a revolutionizing factor; it sets the world in turmoil industrially and politically. The export of capital and the monopolization of the sources of raw materials, being an absolute necessity to an industrially highly-developed nation dominated by Capitalism, the interests of Imperialism become identified with the interests of the nation, interpreted by the ruling class; the government protects and advances these interests through diplomatic means; but a point may be reached where none of the antagonists yield, when the forces of diplomacy no longer reach a temporary solution, and the interests in dispute are put to the arbitrament of the sword. Soldiers slay and destroy, where diplomats intrigued.

The "armed peace" of Imperialism is the expression of the quintessence of capitalist hypocrisy and rapacity. Each nation dreads war, may anxiously attempt to avert war, but all relentlessly and unavoidably pursue a policy that inevitably brings war. The "armed peace" is an expression of the *status quo*; but the *status quo* limits the scope of Imperialism, is itself considered an "aggression," and must be altered by means of war. The horrors of this "armed peace," its torturing uncertainty, dreads and burdens are such that war itself becomes a sort of relief. All Imperialism cloaks itself in the garb of a "civilizing mission," and all Imperialism produces a world catastrophe that drags civilization down to ruin. Imperialism is the brutal and final negation of all the ideal claims of capitalist hypocrisy, expressing the most rapacious projects in all history.

Wars waged under the conditions of imperialistic Capitalism present features of new and epochal significance. They are no longer national wars waged by nations, but international wars waged between groups of nations for international imperialistic purposes; they are wars waged not to preserve the nation but to break through the hampering limits of the nation; they are wars which are determined, not ultimately but immediately, by the economics of productive capacity, and which organize for military purposes the whole of the industrial technology; they are wars which are not simply waged by nations but by peoples, because of a partly actual and largely fictitious interest of all the people in the war, and the pervasive and compulsive ideology of Imperialism; and, finally, they are wars which require and project a rigid centralizing control of the process of industry by the government, the control of State Capitalism, for their prosecution. And it is precisely this State Capitalism, the social characteristic and political expression of Imperialism, that is the distinguishing feature of contemporary capitalist society. This circumstance alone indicates the universal, the fundamental character of Imperialism in relation to Capitalism. But it indicates, simultaneously, the desperate situation of Capitalism. Imperialism is the expression of a stagnant Capitalism, a Capitalism in process of disintegration and verging on collapse.

"The fact that Imperialism means Capitalism in a parasitic or stagnant stage is apparent from the tendency to disintegration which is characteristic of all private ownership of the means of production. The distinction between republican and democratic and monarchist-reactionary imperialistic bourgeoisie is nullified by the fact that both are rotting away while apparently in full bloom (which by no means prevents a striking rapidity of capitalist development in certain branches of industry, or in certain countries, or in certain periods.) In the second place, the decay of Capitalism is characterized by the creation of a huge rentier class, of capitalists who live by 'cutting coupons.' In the four advanced imperialist countries,

33

England, North America, France and Germany, capital, in the form of securities, amounts to 100 or 150 milliards of francs, which involves an annual income of from five to eight milliards per country. In the third place, the export of capital is Capitalism to the second power. In the fourth place, 'finance capital aspires to domination, not to freedom.' Political reaction all along the line is peculiar to Imperialism: bribery, readiness to be purchased, the Panama case in all its forms. In the fifth place, the exploitation of the oppressed nations, indissolubly associated with a policy of annexations, and particularly the exploitation of colonies by a handful of 'great' powers, is progressively transforming the 'civilized' world into a parasite on the backs of hundreds of millions of uncivilized people. The Roman proletarian lived at society's expense. But present-day society lives at the expense of its proletariat. This profound observation of Sismondi has been particularly emphasized by Marx. Imperialism has somewhat changed the situation. The privileged layers of the proletariat of the imperialistic powers are living partly at the expense of the hundreds of millions of uncivilized people. It is evident that Imperialism is dying Capitalism, preparatory to Socialism; that monopoly, which is an *outgrowth* of Capitalism, is *already* the agony of Capitalism, the beginning of the transition to Socialism. The tremendous *socialization* of labor, through Imperialism (which the bourgeois economic apologists call 'the interlocking process') has precisely the same significance ... On the one hand, the tendency of the bourgeoisie and of the opportunists is to transform the richest of the privileged nations into 'permanent' parasites on the body of backward humanity, to 'rest on the laurels' of the exploitation of Negroes, East Indians, etc., holding them in subjection by using the magnificent destructive powers of the newest military technique. On the other hand, the tendency of the *masses*, more oppressed than ever, and burdened with all the torments of imperialistic wars, to cast off this yoke and overthrow the bourgeoisie. In the conflict between these two tendencies, the history of the workers' movement must really begin to move." [8]

The more Imperialism expresses itself as stagnant Capitalism, the more violent will become the struggles of Capitalism to avert its collapse. But a system that must resort to the methods of Imperialism is a system that inevitably strangles itself in its own contradictions. The contradictions of Imperialism are the contradictions of Capitalism, multiplied and aggravated by the corroding stagnation of an economy that historically has persisted beyond its necessity.

A social system is often deceptive in its strength. The war, apparently, marks a strengthening of Capitalism, a new expression of the omnipotence of Capitalism: the state and Capitalism are supreme, control all things with iron despotism. And yet, historically, the war is an expression of the weakness of Capitalism, of its stagnant condition, of the fact that the situation of Capitalism is so desperate as to invoke the use of the most desperate, dangerous means to preserve itself. Imperialism, equally, marks an apparent renewal of the might of Capitalism, a new means for the prolongation of its supremacy. These are facts; but it is a form of renewal and prolongation worse than the disease; that imply new and more desperate struggles, acuter antagonisms, and a multiplication of the factors that produce Imperialism. A still more decrepit Capitalism, an unavoidable limiting of the opportunity for its preservation, – these are the inevitable consequences of the *tendency* of Imperialism.

Imperialism is the final stage of Capitalism: the two are interwoven, persist or collapse as one. The alternative is either the collapse of all civilization, or the coming of Socialism.

Footnotes

1. Imperialism is a specific historical stage of Capitalism. Its peculiarities are threefold: Imperialism means (1) monopolistic Capitalism; (2) parasitic, or stagnant Capitalism; and (3) dying Capitalism ... Imperialism, the most advanced stage of Capitalism in America and Europe, and later of Asia, became fully developed in the

period from 1898 to 1914. The Spanish American War (1898), the Anglo-Boer War (1900-1902), the Russo-Japanese War (1904-1905), and the economic crisis in Europe (1910), are the chief historical milestones of this new era of universal history. – N. Lenin, *Imperialism and the Socialist Schism*, **Sbornik Sotsial-Demokrata**, December 1916.

2. The development and exploitation of the home market mean a revolutionary struggle against Feudalism, – the bourgeois revolution. At the earlier periods of capitalist society, when there was no class conscious proletariat, the bourgeoisie could afford to engage in this revolutionary struggle. But a nation that enters the orbit of capitalist production definitely during the imperialistic epoch pursues a different course. In Russia, for example, the bourgeoisie was afraid to develop intensively its home market, as it meant a revolutionary struggle against Czarism; the bourgeoisie feared this struggle, because it might offer an opportunity to the proletariat and proletarian peasantry to assume power – as has actually been the case. The Russian bourgeoisie, accordingly, dealt gingerly with the home market and sought means of exploitation and accumulation of capital through the control of undeveloped countries Imperialism. This imperialistic character of the Russian bourgeoisie explains many of the events in the Russian Revolution. Where in other countries Imperialism is the product of an over-developed Capitalism, in Russia, as in Japan, it is influenced by an under-developed Capitalism. "In Japan and in Russia," says Lenin, "the monopoly of military power, a measureless extent of territory, or an unusual opportunity to exploit native populations, partly complement and partly replace the monopoly of present-day finance-capital."

3. L.B. Boudin. **Socialism and War**.

4. Monopoly appears in five principal forms: (1) cartells, syndicates and trusts: in these the concentration of production has reached the stage that creates monopolistic leagues of capitalists; (2) the monopoly position of the great banks: three, four or five gigantic banks dominate the entire economic life of America, France and Germany; (3) the conquest of the sources of raw materials by the trust and the financial oligarchy (finance-capital means monopolistic industrial capital united with banking capital); (4) the *beginnings* of the partition of the world (economic) by the international cartells: of such international cartells, controlling the whole world market, and

doing it "amicably" (until war began to redistribute it), there are already more than *one hundred*; the export of capital, a phenomenon distinct from the export of goods under pro-monopolistic Capitalism, is closely allied with the economic and politico-territorial division of the world; (5) the territorial division of the world (colonial era) has been completed. – N. Lenin, *Imperialism and the Socialist Schism*, **loc. cit.**

5. To the landed class ... broad acres and numerous serfs are the most natural expressions of wealth, it conquers and arms to acquire estates. With the development of manufactures and oversea trade, these cruder views are discarded. The landed class retains for a time its hereditary bias to think in terms of actual possession. But little by little the commercial standpoint modifies the attitude ven of the aristocracy. A trading community like Early Victorian England, which can still profitably employ all its capital in its mills and ships, becomes indifferent to the acquisition of territory, and even tends to regard the colonies previously acquired as a useless encumbrance. That was the normal state of mind of our commercial classes during the middle years of last century. They dealt in goods, and in order to sell goods abroad, it was not necessary either to colonize or to conquer. To this phase belongs the typical foreign policy of Liberalism, with its watchwords of peace, non-intervention, and free trade. The third phase, the modern phase, begins when capital has accumulated in large fortunes, when the rate of interest at home begins to fall, and the discovery is made that investments abroad, in unsettled countries with populations more easily exploited than our own, offer swifter and bigger returns. It is the epoch of concession hunting, of coolie labor, of chartered companies, of railway construction, of loans to semi-civilized Powers, of the "opening up" of "dying empires." At this phase the export of capital has become to the ruling class more important and more attractive than the export of goods. The Manchester school disappears, and even Liberals accept Imperialism. – H.N. Brailsford, **The War of Steel and Gold**.

6. The early Imperialism of the United States, externally, was largely a reflex of the Monroe Doctrine. Originally promulgated as a bulwark of the new Republic, the Monroe Doctrine, as American Capitalism developed, was transformed into an imperialistic instrument, the definite impetus in this direction being given by President Cleveland, and completed by President Roosevelt. American capital and

enterprises were established in Central America and the Caribbeans, the result being the creation of a *de facto* empire, based upon the financial control which ultimately leads to political domination. In his Mobile speech in 1913 President Wilson opposed granting oil concessions to non-American promoters by the weaker American states, as the granting of these concessions was a menace to the Monroe Doctrine, Here was formulated completely the imperialistic phase of the Monroe Doctrine, not intended to protect the political independence of the American continents against foreign aggression, but to aggrandize, financially, economically and politically, the Imperialism of the United States as against the other nations of the world. The rapacious expression of this doctrine is shown in the complete subjection of the Republics of Central America and the Caribbeans, completed and consolidated during the "liberal" administration of Woodrow Wilson. This administration tried to project a Pan-Americanism in the interest of American Imperialism, the chief purpose of which was to secure economic and governmental stability, as, in the words of Mr. Wilson, "revolution tears up the very roots of everything that makes life go steadily forward and the light grow from generation to generation." This "Pan-Americanism" is, in a measure, an off-shoot of the Monroe Doctrine; but it is a contradiction, for as long as the Monroe Doctrine prevails, which is a strictly national doctrine, any attempt at Pan-Americanism is simply a scheme to promote the Imperialism of the United States. This Pan-Americanism and the Monroe Doctrine are merging into the definite continental expression of American Imperialism.

7. The "trade" of Morocco, if by that word is meant the exchange of European manufactured goods against the raw produce of its agriculture, is at the best inconsiderable ... What matters in Morocco is the wealth of its virgin mines ... A German firm, the Mannesmann Brothers, could indeed boast that it had obtained an exclusive concession to work all the mines of Morocco in return for money which it had lent to an embarrassed Sultan during its civil wars. That this was the real issue is proved by the terms which were more than once discussed between Paris and Berlin for the settlement of the dispute. A "*détente*," or provisional settlement of the dispute was concluded in 1910, which had only one clause that German finance would share with French finance in the various undertakings and companies which aimed at "opening up" Morocco by ports, railways, mines, and other public works. No effect was ever given to this

undertaking, and German irritation at the delays of French diplomacy and French finance culminated in the dispatch of the gunboat *Panther* to Agadir as a prelude to further "conversations." – H.N. Brailsford, **The War of Steel and Gold**.

8. N. Lenin, *Imperialism and the Socialist Schism*, **loc. cit.** Another passage from this article will prove instructive:

"Our definition of Imperialism puts us in opposition to Karl Kautsky, who refuses to accept Imperialism as 'a phase of Capitalism,' and defines Imperialism as the *policy* 'favored by' finance-capital, as the tendency of the 'industrial' countries to annex 'agrarian' countries. This definition of Kautsky's is theoretically all wrong. The peculiarity of Imperialism is the hegemony, precisely not of industrial, but of financial capital, the tendency to annex, not agrarian, but any countries at all. Kautsky *tears* the policy of Imperialism from its economy, severs monopolism in economy from monopolism in policy in order to pave the way for his base bourgeois reformism of 'disarmament,' 'ultra-Imperialism,' and other follies. This theoretical misrepresentation is completely cal culatod to obliterate the profound contradictions of Imperialism, and thus to prepare the theory of 'unity' with the apologists of Imperialism, the outright social patriots and opportunists."

Chapter III
Class Divisions Under Imperialism

THE epoch of Imperialism expresses a readjustment in the concentration of capital and industry, and the radical alteration of class relations and the form of expression of class interests.

The accumulation of capital produces the concentration of industry, and the concentration of industry accelerates the accumulation of capital. The development of technology requires larger and larger industrial units; the battle of competition, waged through the cheapening of commodities, places the small producer at a disadvantage and encourages concentrated industrial enterprises. A simple industry becomes complex: the steel industry not only manufactures steel, but by-products, and acquires mines and railways. In this process of concentration, the smaller capitalists are either driven to the wall, compelled to unite their capitals, or forced into new lines of industrial endeavor, where the development of technology and the battle of competition again produce concentration. The consequences of this activity are the decay of the industrial middle class and a development toward monopoly.

The process of concentration of industry is accompanied by the centralization of capital. Normally, the centralization of capital is a consequence of concentration of industry; actually, it may be and often is its cause. Centralization [1] is financial, the unity of many small or large capitals used co-operatively and not competitively. Centralization may precede concentration of industry, accelerate concentration, and plays an important part in capitalist development. "The world would still be without railroads if it had been obliged to wait until accumulation should have enabled a few individual capitalists to undertake the construction of a railroad. Centralization, on the other hand, accomplished this by a turn of the hand through stock companies." [2] Centralization strips capital of the fetters of its isolation and unites it into a formidable instrument of development and exploitation, reproducing many-fold the value of the totality of its individual components; through this unity, centralization makes possible enterprises before which the individual capitals would shrink in terror or impotence; it accelerates economic expansion, breaks new ground, and paves the way for systematic, intensive exploitation and development. Centralization in the United States built great railway systems, the tentacles of which, so to say, smothered the barbaric isolation and virility of the great West, opening a new continent to the civilizing beneficence of capitalist industry, profit and religion. Centralization forged the tools which tapped the great natural resources, drawing the whole of our continent into the circle of capitalist exploitation; it gave impetus to new industries and provided the means with which to build up new industries. If this process was accompanied by concentration of industry and economic efficiency, that was partial and incidental – technically inevitable, but subjectively incidental.

In the capitalist order of things, accordingly, centralization performed a mighty work. Speculative centralization accomplished with almost lightning rapidly what planful, systematic effort would have by now barely started. The process of speculative centralization, however, becomes a fetter upon the systematic, co-ordinated concentration of industry; produces a large amount of waste, makes dominantly the speculative capitalist instead of the industrial capitalist the arbiter of industry, and converts industry into an expression of finance instead of finance into an expression of industry. Necessary at an earlier epoch, centralization becomes a fetter upon the industrial process, and industry re-adjusts itself, standardizes and specializes itself in accord with the integration of production. The extensive or expansive exploitation of the epoch of centralization is succeeded by re-adjustment and intensive development. The ultimate aim of centralization is monopoly, and for a time monopoly prevails. But while competition produces monopoly, monopoly produces

42

competition on a higher plane and within narrower limits, between million-capitals. However, the attempt at the monopolistic management of industry is seen as unwieldy, inefficient, wasteful, and as defeating its own purpose. There is a revolt [3] at the attempt of monopolistic finance to direct the technique of industry. Monopolistic *industry* does not succeed in maintaining its ascendancy, but monopolistic *finance* becomes dominant. Financial capital does not direct the technique of industry, but it controls the industrial forces.

The attempt at indiscriminate monopoly, moreover, acts as a fetter upon the concentration and integration of industry. Competition cannot be wiped out completely through struggle and rivalry; this may be accomplished through co-operation. Under these conditions, the typical industry of concentrated capital becomes the steel industry, as in the United States.

The Steel Trust did not attempt to crush all its rivals and secure a complete monopoly. This trust and the independents maintain friendly relations and co-operate, although, of course, the trust dominates, and all are still further dominated by finance-capital. The policy becomes general. It becomes general because of the compulsion of industrial necessity; and it becomes general, moreover, because the development of the home market no longer allows indiscriminate competition, and because the unity of capitalist interests is necessary in the struggles of Imperialism for investment markets and new spheres of development. The accumulation of capital has up to this point proceeded, in a measure, through the expropriation of one capitalist by another within the nation; it now becomes dominantly a process of one national group of capitalists expropriating a rival group through control of industrial development in undeveloped countries, and by successful competition in the other markets of the world. The unity of a national Capitalism is indispensable under these conditions.

Industrial concentration does not cease at this point; on the contrary, it is given a new impetus, assumes a new form and becomes more systematic and co-ordinated, more strictly industrial and technological in character. The energy of industry is freed to specialize and standardize its process and production, increasing output and decreasing costs. It is precisely this specialization and standardization that make American Capitalism a most successful competitor in the markets of the world. Moreover, through the integrating activity of State Capitalism, industry acquires a new and more complete form of concentration, the control of the state imposing adaptation and unity, and regulating the relations of industry to industry. The control of the state means the climax of industrial concentration, precisely as State Capitalism and Imperialism mean the climax of Capitalism itself. This development proceeds under the sway of finance-capital: the whole of industry comes under the domination of monopolistic finance, and subservient to its policy, – including the state itself, openly and unashamed. The ventures of Imperialism are carried on through finance-capital; these ventures are indispensable to the life of capitalist industry at the climax of its development; and finance-capital, accordingly, becomes the dictator of the industrial forces of a nation.

The monopoly and domination of finance-capital are not disputed, since the export of capital is now the nerve-center of capitalist production and expansion. The industrial capitalist becomes subservient to the financial capitalist because exports are necessary to him, and under the conditions of trade today the export of products must be financed by the export of capital. James A. Farrell, president of the United States Steel Corporation, recently emphasized the necessity of the export of capital, of foreign investments, as "a commercial preparedness measure," as the means of increasing trade and exports by financing the needs of the growing countries "which are America's best customers." Great Britain's $20,000,000,000 of foreign investments, according to Farrell, "retain and strengthen its hold on the neutral markets of the world." Through the development of technology and the increased productivity of

44

labor, the mass of surplus products steadily accumulates; the industrial capitalist must dispose of these products through export trade; the demand for these products must be stimulated through the development of the internal markets of undeveloped countries, which is accomplished through investments and the export of means of production; and, accordingly, the export of products becomes in large measure dependent upon the export of capital. This being the situation, capitalist industry rallies to Imperialism as necessary to its existence, prosperity and expansion.

The investments which are the animating factor of Imperialism are, as stated previously, an industrial as much as a financial transaction. The capital invested in an undeveloped country is used to build railways, factories, docks, irrigation systems, to exploit mines, etc.; all this requires steel, machinery and other products, including skilled labor; and when American finance-capital, say, invests in Mexico to build railways, it is tacitly or openly agreed that the bulk of the necessary materials shall be purchased in the United States. This is the rule in all such enterprises. There is here a double profit, a profit on the investment, directly, which goes to finance-capital; and a profit on the export of materials, indirectly, which goes to the industrial capitalist. This is a circumstance which converts Imperialism, essentially a mechanism of finance-capital, into the concern of *all capitalist groups*, the export of capital being the purveyor, stabilizer and guarantor of profit generally [4]; and this results in a unity of capitalist interests that is a distinguishing feature of the era of Imperialism. The domination of finance-capital is assured because it becomes the typical expression of Capitalism.

In this process, the industrial middle-class, the small and middle-sized producer, disappears as an independent factor. Turned into an anachronism through the concentration of industry, the small producer fights desperately against the process; but concentration becomes steadily ascendant. The industrial middle class may use its electoral strength, in

45

conjunction with workers whom it has cajoled, to strike at concentrated industry by means of legislative action. But, gradually, the fight ends. It ends not only because concentrated capital is supreme, but because the new era of Imperialism cannot tolerate this division of energy within the capitalist class. A compromise is struck – the remnants of the industrial middle class, together with the producers in between the middle class and big industry, are allowed to exist and to participate in the profits of Imperialism, in return for which this class ceases its struggles for independence. It straggles along dependent upon finance-capital, its miserable petty bourgeois soul bought and paid for by the master. And under these conditions, the remnants of the industrial *petite bourgeoise* become a repulsively reactionary factor, more imperialistic than imperialistic finance itself, where formerly pluming itself in the colors of freedom, democracy, and even revolution! This compromise is equally struck between trust and independent competitors – concerns of million-capital, which are not part of the industrial middle class, but which previously acted against big capital through competition; a situation, moreover, which is in itself partly determined by the circumstance that there are certain historical limits to industrial concentration and the expropriation of one capitalist by another under the technological, social and political conditions of Capitalism. Harmony, as much as is possible in a system where dog eats dog, prevails, and all seek recompense for the concessions of compromise in the fabulous profits of Imperialism.

But now a factor emerges of prime social importance – the creation of a new middle class. The differences between the old and the new middle class may be summarized, – the old was industrial, an owning class, the new is social, an income class; the old was independent, the new dependent; the old was determined by the conditions of its existence in a struggle against the concentration of industry, the new is the product of concentrated industry and its obedient vassal. The upper layer of this new middle class consists of individuals owning shares in concentrated industry. It is not an industrial factor, having been expropriated from direct control of industry, and its financial interests in trusts and corporations are not of a character to insure domination. The lower layer consists of managers, superintendents, engineers, technicians, and professional men of specialized training for industrial pursuits. These various elements are wholly dependent upon concentrated capital and its imperialistic manifestations, – the upper layer, because of its dividends; the lower, because it occupies a privileged status in industry, and because a feature of Imperialism is the export of technical skill to undeveloped countries to manage and superintend the industries created there by the investment of capital. This new middle class is thoroughly reactionary, although it develops a peculiar type of "liberal ideas."

An adjunct of this new middle class, and trying to force itself within its ranks, is a certain category of ordinary skilled labor. In the development of the internal market of an undeveloped country, skilled labor is necessary, and this skilled labor, clearly, cannot be secured in the country being developed. There occurs, accordingly, the export of a mass of skilled workers – clerks, stenographers, mechanics, etc. – all of whom are dependent directly upon Imperialism and become its prophets in more or less conscious degree.

The character of strength and danger inherent in Imperialism flows from precisely this circumstance, that it seduces hitherto liberal and oppositional elements, organizes them into the social and psychological army of Imperialism. By means of innumerable visible and invisible threads of interest and dependency, finance-capital bends to its will and purpose the whole of capitalist society. It reigns supreme. Imperialism accomplishes that which never prevailed hitherto, the complete domination of capitalist autocracy in its most revolting form; and it manages, moreover, at least temporarily, to scatter the opposition to chaff, – except the potential opposition of the revolutionary industrial proletariat.

47

Imperialism accomplishes another determining thing: it brings the "labor movement" into its service. At this stage, Imperialism becomes specially interested in the psychology and action of the working class. In the struggles of Imperialism, a national Capitalism must present a united front. The unity of capitalist interests becomes imperative, as any material division of energy through unbridled rivalry of interests weakens the economic, political and military power of the nation. The unity of the various layers of the capitalist class has been secured partly through compromise, largely through their subordination to and dependence upon monopolistic finance-capital. But this unity is incomplete unless it includes the workers. Industrial regularity and efficiency are indispensable in the international competition of Imperialism, equally during peace and war, and a discontented class of workers becomes exceedingly unpleasant and perhaps dangerous. Monopolistic finance-capital secures support for its imperialistic adventures among the other layers of the capitalist class by a "distribution" of the profits of Imperialism; and this policy is extended to groups of skilled labor, their support being secured by means of higher wages, steady employment, better hours and conditions of work generally, and legislative measures conferring status upon skilled labor. The tendency is to create a homogeneity of interests, which is largely, if temporarily, successful. Skilled labor, sensing its importance and opportunity, makes the attempt through its unions to secure even larger concessions, and establish for itself a place in the governing system of the nation. It rejects the general class struggle against Capitalism, and acts as a caste the psychology and action of which are determined by the aspiration to absorb itself in the ruling system of things. The general process creates a reactionary mass whose interests are promoted by the more intense exploitation of the proletariat of average, unskilled labor, the overwhelming mass of the workers, and by imperialistic adventures.

The governmental form of expression of this development is State Capitalism. [5] The unity of class and group interests must be and is maintained and conserved by the authority of the state. The end of economic individualism is symbolized by governmental control of industry and conditions of labor; the state, moreover, acts directly to intensify the concentration of industry and "regulate" the revolts of labor.

The industrial units in the nation under State Capitalism are no longer allowed to proceed without being co-ordinated to the general process of national industry and its international interests. Representative institutions become more and more incapable of coping with the new and vast industrial requirements; parliamentary government virtually breaks down; and governmental power becomes centralized in the control of administrative autocrats. The state becomes an actual factor in industry through control, regulation and direction. This represents, moreover, a new form of State Capitalism. The older and the newer State Capitalism differ in this, that while the two may merge into each other, the first is pre-imperialistic and consists simply in government ownership of certain industries, while the newer State Capitalism is imperialistic, may not actually own any industry, but exercises drastic and despotic control over the general industrial process.

The older State Capitalism was an expression of competitive Capitalism, an expression largely of a weakening industrial middle class that conceived government ownership as a means of destroying the trusts and certain of its industrial oppressors; while imperialistic State Capitalism is essentially an expression of industrial collectivism, finance-capital and Imperialism, − in short, of Capitalism at the climax of its development. It is not necessary, it is even undesirable, that imperialistic State Capitalism should have any actual government ownership of industry; it is sufficient that it co-ordinate, concentrate and control the process of industry, and express the unity of capitalist interests, compelling this unity by state force if necessary. Imperialism and State Capitalism [6], accordingly, represent a new epoch in Capitalism, and a radical alteration in the relations of classes and in the form of expression of their class interests.

A vital fact of State Capitalism is that skilled labor becomes a part of the governing system. The unions which comprise the aristocracy of labor gradually acquire an influence in State Capitalism, a concession that is offered them as a bribe, and which they accept, at least temporarily, uniting their forces with Imperialism. Skilled labor having been seduced, the proletariat of average, unskilled labor becomes the revolutionary force. The covert and overt clash between skilled and unskilled labor, which even hitherto has been a prime factor, now assumes a more definite and violent aspect. The two groups engage in an open, bitter struggle, as in order to secure and retain its privileges skilled labor completely abandons and betrays the unskilled; indeed, it is part of the tacit agreement implied in Laborism becoming a part of State Capitalism that it shall use its influence to maintain unskilled labor in subjection. During a war this function of Laborism becomes particularly necessary. In January, 1918, while the workers were engaging in revolutionary strikes and demonstrations in Germany, the unions of skilled labor acted in favor of the government. The great western strikes in this country, in the spring and summer of 1917, were an expression of unskilled labor, a spontaneous revolt acting through mass action equally against the employers and the "regular" unions. The bureaucracy of the American Federation of Labor acted against these strikes and generally betrayed them. The strikes coalesced around the Industrial Workers of the World, and the AF of L actively engaged in the fight against the IWW.

"Accumulation of capital," says Marx, "is increase of the proletariat." Imperialism increases the proletariat by bringing new regions and its human raw material within the circle of capitalist exploitation. This new proletariat, naturally, is expropriated and becomes the starting point of a new capitalist accumulation; it is, moreover, a proletariat of average, unskilled labor, the required skilled labor being largely, if not exclusively, imported. There occurs a repetition of the struggle

50

between skilled and unskilled, with this difference, that the struggle is at the same time intensified and obscured by national and racial prejudice. The conditions of this newly-created proletariat are as abominable as in the initial period of the industrial revolution in England. Children are mercilessly driven and flogged if they lag; men and women are worked from 14 to 20 hours a day, generally seven days a week; wages are frightfully low; fraud is general, and when the workers rebel they usually demand the day's wage in advance; and a sort of peonage is imposed that is vile and degrading. The untutored mind of these people must indeed consider the blessings of civilization as peculiar! The profits on investments are, naturally, very high. Capital recoups itself for the concessions made to skilled labor by an intensified national and international exploitation of the unskilled. This creates a class of average labor that is truly international in its misery and exploitation, and which develops the material conditions and ideology for international revolution.

Upon the misery and exploitation of unskilled labor, the overwhelming mass of the industrial proletariat, the new *bloc* of general reactionary interests thrives and becomes prosperous. But unskilled labor awakens to a consciousness of its misery and its strength. The revolts of the unskilled become more numerous and more general. It becomes the immediate and potential revolutionary force against Capitalism, and through its action the *bloc* of reactionary interests is broken. It is through the interests and action of the proletariat of average, unskilled labor, the dominant form of labor in modern industry, that the Social Revolution will come.

Footnotes

1. The word "centralization" throughout this discussion it used to indicate a financial category, the word "concentration" an industrial category, although in practice the two are not rigidly separable.

2. Karl Marx, **Capital**, Vol.1, Chapter XXV, Section 2.

3. Certain developments in railway history may illustrate this fact. The New Haven transportation system, under the control of President Mellen, adopted the policy of monopolizing New England's transportation system. Mellen sacrificed and lowered dividends and efficiency, acquired control of competing water lines, bought up trolley systems, grasped railroad lines far beyond the New Haven's field of operations, and paid exorbitant prices for virtually useless properties, all to develop a monopoly; a process that, as one financial paper put it, "can only be justified in the event of monopoly being established to an extent that will permit monopolistic rates to be charged." In 1913 the Mellen regime was overthrown, without a murmur from its dominating influence, the Morgan financial empire. E.H. Harriman tried in a measure the same process, and after his death the railway systems he had united split apart. But the animating instinct of these men was right: the railway systems had to be integrated; it could not, however, be accomplished through private initiative alone, but it is now being accomplished through the medium of state control, which, by guaranteeing dividends, may eliminate wasteful competition and manage the railways as an integral system, in accord with industrial requirements.

4. The organization of the American International Corporation was the sign and symbol of awakening to the opportunity of seizing world power, backed up by a vigorous propaganda for mightier armaments. This International Corporation represents the great interests of finance-capital, and of such powerful economic units as the steel industry. Its purpose is to seek out investment markets, exploit and control them. It is a definite expression of the new era in American trade an era of systematic export of products organized by the export of capital. Its capitalization of $50,000,000 is purely nominal, a mere bagatelle in comparison with the millons upon millons controlled by its sponsors. It is around the activity of this corporation, in China, in Chile, anywhere an opportunity offers, that American Imperialism is organizing itself ... What are the economic facts ... that lie at the roots of our developing Imperialism? The credit balance of American foreign trade from the outbreak of the war to January 31, 1917, represents a huge total of $5,574,000,000 ... The statistics are not significant because of what they express in foreign trade alone. Trade in itself is not a cause of belligerency between nations today ... The outstanding fact is that America, from a debtor nation, *has become a creditor nation*. Two years ago American Capitalism owed the world

more than two billion dollars; today the world owes America nearly three billion dollars. Where this country previously imported masses of capital, today it is exporting capital, and is developing the power to export it in still larger masses. The loans to the belligerent governments, paying good interest, represent a financial reserve for the future. And these loans are steadily increasing – at present they amount to more than $2,500,000,000 ... The export of American capital to Mexico, and to Central and South America generally, has been the factor in the development of Imperialism in this country, with its menace to peace and freedom at home and abroad. How much more menacing will this Imperialism become when the export of capital assumes larger dimensions! – Louis C. Fraina, *The War and America*, in **The Class Struggle**, May-June 1917.

5. The belligerent nations are instituting State Capitalism by the absorption of economic activity within the control of the state. This was impossible in a society of isolated small-scale production; it is possible and practicable only in a society in which industry is highly-developed, in which that concentration of industry prevails which is a distinguishing feature of the accumulation of capital and imperialism. State and nation are no longer organized as competing military powers, but as basically competing economic groups. The vital significance of this State Capitalism is that it is not a temporary expedient of military necessity, but the culmination of a previous tendency toward State Capitalism as the inexorable expression of Imperialism, and of which war itself is a product. In previous wars the state simply taxed or seized property for its purposes; now it is compelled to seize upon the whole of industry and re-organize through State Capitalism the productive forces of a nation. The change is tremendous and fundamental.

6. The State Capitalism of Germany is a merging of the old and new, and is consequently not typical of imperialistic State Capitalism, being burdened with many of the evils of government ownership and operation. The countries adopting State Capitalism are aware of these evils, and try to avoid them. At a meeting of the Liverpool Section of the British Chemical Society, reported in **The Journal of the Society of Chemical Industry**, November 15, 1917, Mr. A.T. Smith lamented the "invasion of the official" incident to rigid State Capitalism: "... time is largely occupied in attempting to comply with the wishes of these various new departments. It may be that this condition of affairs

is inseparable from the control of manufacturers by a central department or departments in London, but I venture to suggest that rites and ordinances have been multiplied to an unnecessary degree ... Centralization is all very well in its way, but I venture to suggest that too much centralization in a trade like ours is worse than useless." In the discussion, a speaker emphasized the problem, and declared it was interesting to read in a report of the German Iron and Steel Institute a condemnation of the methods of "organization" in the industry – the writer complaining of a "superabundance of government departments." The United States has not had the older forms of State Capitalism, consequently its imperialistic State Capitalism avoids its evils – it establishes government control of industry, but not operation or ownership. The state controls, concentrates and co-ordinates, but operation remains with private capitalist initiative. The **New York Tribune**, in its issue of December 28, 1917, editorializing on the government's assumption of railroad control, aptly posed the problem: "If the government will stop there [state control] and leave the operation of the railroads in the hands of operating men, the effectiveness of the transportation machine will be increased. If, having taken control of the railroads out of the hands of the owners, it will hand them back to the operating people and say, 'There they are; take them and run them as one system, without thought of dividends and interest payments, using every mile of track and locomotive in common, only to get the freight moved' – if it will say that, the thing is done. The railroads will have been 'unified.' That is essential." Imperialistic State Capitalism bends the state directly to its purposes; state control of industry is indirectly control of the state by industry.

54

Chapter IV
The Death of Democracy

THE conditions of Imperialism and State Capitalism generate a reactionary trend, nationally and internationally. The reactionary and brutalizing character of Imperialism does not consist simply in the fact that it produces war and crushes the independence of peoples. Imperialism strikes equally at independence and democracy within the nation, at the paltry democracy of Capitalism: it means the end of the era of bourgeois democracy. [1]

The democracy of the bourgeoisie, historically, consists of political freedom and the recognition of the rights of the individual, – the ideology of the era of free competition, of *laissez-faire*. In this democracy, freedom of action is a cardinal social principal. That government is considered best which governs least. Bourgeois democracy is, on the one hand, a reaction against the hierarchical rigidity of Feudalism, and on the other, an expression of the economic individualism of free competition which is the distinguishing feature of Capitalism in its pre-imperialistic stages, – the democracy of the individual, independent production and exchange of commodities. But as industry concentrates and annihilates free competition, the ideolology of democracy and of individual independence is displaced by the ideology of domination. The fact may be disguised by prattle about the interests of the collectivity and social control; it is, nevertheless, a reaction against bourgeois democracy.

In this reaction against democracy, industrial facts are the compulsive force. The larger and more integrated the industrial units become, the more necessary is the subordination of the individual to the technological process. There is a lessening of the individuality of the worker in industry; the technological development progressively renders individual skill and independence less necessary, except in the case of a privileged group of skilled technicians and managers. An essential characteristic of concentrated industry is that it multiplies the mass of average, unskilled workers, and deadens their individuality and intelligence in so far as the technical process is concerned. Labor, in the measure that it is specialized and standardized, becomes mechanical. This circumstance develops contempt in the upper class, and a growing disregard of the "rights" of these workers. The general reactionary tendency in education and the campaign for technical education in the public schools are, largely, a more or less conscious appreciation of the fact that a general and increasing intelligence is no longer necessary in the mass of labor; mechanical aptitude for a particular kind of work takes its place. In its earlier period, the factory system required and developed the general intelligence of the workers: out of this fact arose compulsory education; today, the factory system negates intelligence in the mass of workers.

Moreover, as industry develops, internationalizes itself and Imperialism arises, the democracy of *laissez-faire* is considered as interfering with industrial efficiency and the mobilization of national power, and is incontinently discarded. Democracy, to the bourgeoisie, was a means to an end: the overthrow of Feudalism and the development of the supremacy of Capitalism. Arrived at maturity of development, Capitalism liberates itself from the ideology of democracy in the measure that it realizes autocracy may more effectively promote its interests. The state, accordingly, acquires new and widening powers; the ideology of free competition, that that government is best which governs least, is substituted by the concept that that government is best which governs most, which controls the forces of society rigidly and autocratically – in the interest, of course, of dominant Capitalism! But this transformation in the state is not comprised simply in the widening of its functions, but in a radical alteration of its procedure. Parallel with the acquisition of new industrial functions, the state acquires a new procedure, the procedure of absolutism, and becomes an autocracy cloaked in the cloak of democratic forms. The Roman Republic was still democratic in appearance for decades after it had become autocratic in actuality.

Capitalism today subordinates everything to the success of its imperialistic adventures. Autocracy, not the autocracy of a Czaristic Russia, but the autocracy of an industrially organized, imperialistic Germany, is much more speedy and efficient in action than democracy, and, moreover, more tractable to the interests of a ruling caste. Government having engaged itself to promote finance-capital in its imperialistic projects, it becomes increasingly un-democratic. In the struggles of Imperialism, the resort to force is the ultimate deciding factor. A strong government is indispensable – which means an autocratically centralized government, a mighty militarism, and the intensive subordination of the general will to the requirements of the ruling class. The spirit of militarism becomes the animating spirit of the state, in its political and industrial action. There is this vital similarity between militarism and State Capitalism, that each depends upon a coerced sense of discipline, a moral and physical regimentation of the masses. The actual procedure of government becomes autocratic where formerly it was oligarchic. The power of the state is centralized in its administrative, and not its legislative, department. The Chief Executive of a nation, whether President, Prime Minister or Emperor, becomes vested with the functions of dictator. The Strong Man policy dominates throughout society [2], and particularly toward the activity of the industrial proletariat, the subjection of which becomes increasingly indispensable.

This autocratic tendency is strengthened by the proConsul system of government that an imperialistic nation imposes upon its over-seas possessions and "protectorates." The pro-Consul rules with an iron hand, exclusively in the interests of the ruling class of his own government; democracy, decency, honesty, all are complacently discarded, and a moral and physical reign of terror instituted to maintain "undeveloped" peoples in subjugation. A brutal and brutalizing mercenary soldiery becomes the guardian of the holy sanctuary of capitalist civilization and profits, – particularly profits. The Strong Man policy is necessary in these imperialistic possessions, and it reacts and stimulates a similar policy at home. Imperialism is international and its policy of repression is international. The rights of the individual, particularly the mythical rights of the workers, become a fetter upon the sway and development of capital, and are crushed. Efficiency, in the imperialistic sense, industrial and political, is the measure by which all things are tested. The reactionary trend becomes general and all-pervasive.

All layers of the ruling class acquiesce in this reaction, the *petite bourgeoisie* [3], and the new middle class. The bureaucratic system which is an expression of this reactionary trend in government draws its material largely from these groups. The export of bureaucrats to foreign possessions becomes an important source of employment and revenue for members of the middle class, and they sing hosannas to the new imperialistic dispensation. The opportunity of making a career is enlarged for the sons of the *petite bourgeoisie* through the military and civil service in colonial territory. In various ways, financial, industrial, social and political, the middle and the lower layers of the ruling class are seduced by the policy of Imperialism, become its most reactionary and brutal adherents.

The development of Capitalism, jointly with the widening of collegiate educational opportunity, has created an intellectual proletariat, workers of the brain. National Capitalism, for a time, absorbs these "intellectuals." But a stage arrives when there is a real over-production of this class of workers. Temporarily, their imagination is intrigued by liberal social movements, and, occasionally, by Socialism. But inevitably, if gradually, their petty bourgeois souls scent the flesh-pots of Imperialism, and they become its prophets. These "workers of the brain," the surplus which is not absorbed internally, are exported to colonial possessions and "spheres of influence," where the growing industrial and social development provides opportunity for their services. As the production of these intellectuals increases, turned out by our institutions of learning as a factory turns out hats and shoes, and largely standardized, new fields must be conquered to absorb this particular commodity, and they proclaim the mission of their "superior race" to spread the blessings of civilization, and incidentally of the factory system and the intellectuals, among the backward races.

In every imperialistic country, it is precisely these "workers of the brain" who manufacture and carry into the ranks of the workers the ideology and the enthusiasm of Imperialism. These intellectuals, which the older Socialism expected would become a mighty ally of the proletarian revolution, are a corrupt and corrupting social force. They constitute an insidiously dangerous force, moreover, as they disguise the sordid schemes of Imperialism in the beauty of science, civilization, and progress generally. These intellectuals, like the plague, are a contamination everywhere; but they are particularly numerous and group-conscious in Germany, where they constitute the intellectual army of Imperialism. In **Bismarck's Erbe**, Prof. Hans Delbrück frankly states the needs of this class: "What must give our colonies their specific character is the upper layer, the thousands of graduates of our higher and intermediate educational institutions which are being constantly produced by our fine school-system, for whose talents there is, however, no suitable employment at home ... These we must send into the world as engineers, merchants, planters, physicians, superintendents, officers, to rule the great masses of the inferior races, as the English are doing in India. Such a colonial-Germany will not only rise to the position of World Power, but will, at the same time, solve our most difficult social problem the finding of suitable employment for the rising sons of the people, the surplus of intelligence which finds no proper field of activity at home." The "*intellectuals*" of Germany were intense and brutal adherents of the war; while the socially different *intelligentsia* of Russia was an active counter-revolutionary force in the proletarian revolution.

59

Incidentally, it is interesting to observe that a phase of these developments is an intellectual reaction. Pragmatism becomes the philosophy of "liberal" Imperialism, and Bergsonism the philosophy of State Capitalism. The one tests all things by the test of practice, of social efficiency, degraded by the miserable bourgeois soul into the degrading utilitarian philosophy of "results" ; the other expresses, in a philosophy in which reactionary and liberal ideas jostle each other, fusing into a system essentially of reaction, that unity of divergent class interests which characterizes the epoch of State Capitalism, camouflaging itself in the colors of radical and intellectual democracy. The philosopher enters the service of the imperialist.

In matters that directly concern Imperialism and State Capitalism, philosophy is reactionary; in other matters, and where necessary to deceive, it is radically liberal. It is this latter circumstance which produces the deception that the new era intellectually is progressive. The developments in science and philosophy of a progressive character, which are inevitable, are degraded to the purposes of the ruling class. Even in its progressive aspects the new philosophy serves reactionary purposes: the progressive concept that the child's mental development is furthered by the use of the hands and of tools becomes transformed into a means of turning out good, average industrial operatives; the radical hypothesis, that the pragmatic test is the ultimate test of philosophy and of practice, becomes transformed into the doctrine that what is, is right, that results are the supreme consideration, and the creation of a new social god, the totem-god of Efficiency. It is this circumstance that explains the contradiction of a "liberal" social thinker promoting and justifying a brutal and brutalizing State Capitalism. Socially, within limits that are rigidly definite and that promote the interests of Capital, Imperialism and State Capitalism may be progressive; politically, economically and internationally, Imperialism and State Capitalism are compellingly reactionary.

Radical and liberal social movements merge and develop into a new "progressivism." This progressivism is an ally of Imperialism, promotes and is itself promoted by Imperialism. The liberal ideas and social reform program of progressivism proceed within limits which not only do not hamper Imperialism, but directly promote its growth and ascendancy. The liberal Lloyd-George becomes the director and dictator of the war of an Imperialism that formerly considered him its worst enemy. The characteristics of this new progressivism are typical in the United States, where they have acquired definite expression. [4] The various progressive movements of the decaying middle class meet defeat after defeat, and then disaster. The social alignment changes. Where the old progressivism coalesced around the Democratic Party, historically the party of the small bourgeoisie, the new progressivism develops within the Republican Party, historically the party of Big Capital and Imperialism. The enunciation of the "New Nationalism" by Theodore Roosevelt in 1912 marked an epoch in American politics. It was a clear and consistent formulation of the requirements of the new era of concentrated industry and collectivistic Capitalism. It called for the extension of the functions of the Federal government, regulation equally of capital and labor, the Strong Man policy of administrative centralization of the powers of the state, and the necessity of co-ordinating and unifying all the forces of the capitalist class through the national administrative control of industry, – in all essentials, imperialistic State Capitalism. The "New Nationalism" included a series of social reforms and progressive measures typical of the social and political requirements of Imperialism. During the war, Roosevelt enunciated a new doctrine, the "Larger Americanism," which, basing itself upon the program of the "New Nationalism," developed and promoted an aggressive foreign policy as a necessary means of promoting the international imperialistic interests of the United States. This progressivism is rampantly militaristic and imperialistic: at the three major party conventions in 1916, the convention of the Progressive Party was most decidedly militaristic and aggressive, bitterly criticizing the "pacific" policy of President Wilson. This progressivism barters away its ideals and independence for a share in the spoils of Imperialism. [5] The reaction against democracy has been a characteristic feature of the United States for the past fifty years. The Civil War and its aftermath of industrial expansion marked the doom of the older democracy. The dictatorship of the Federal government during the administration of Lincoln persisted into the administration of Grant, and in latent or open form became thereafter a feature of the American government. The corruption in politics, and the miserable petty stature of the men elected to Congress, developed popular contempt of the national legislature, and correspondingly strengthened the powers of the Presidency. The actual functions of government were assumed by the executive, while the legislature dickered for partisan political advantages and waged royal fights over the "pork barrel." President Roosevelt brutally and contemptuously terrorized Congress. President Wilson made Congress subservient to his will in all things. The despotism of the judiciary emphasized the despotism of the Presidency. The centralization and autocracy of industry expressed itself in the centralization and autocracy of government. By a process of terrorism and ingenious fraud the right to the franchise was extensively limited. Democracy was trampled upon mercilessly, particularly during strikes.

In government, as in industry, autocracy is dominant. All this proceeds simultaneously with the introduction of a sham democracy operating through a variety of schemes that temporarily deceives the masses. But only temporarily: the mailed fit too often smashes through this sham democracy and exposes the sinister autocracy and brutality that direct the nation.

The death of democracy, of bourgeois democracy, and the intensified struggle against the oncoming proletarian democracy of communist Socialism, are the necessary products of Imperialism and State Capitalism. Why is this particularly characteristic of the United States? There are three typically imperialistic nations, each emphasizing a particular phase of the new era. Great Britain, – which typifies Imperialism as developed upon the basis of an old established colonial dominion; Germany, – typifying the nation trying to establish its Imperialism by systematic aggression and rapine among a world of imperialistic rivals; and the United States, – typifying the nation within whose borders Imperialism has most actively established itself, drastically developing the internal conditions of Imperialism. The Imperialism of Great Britain and Germany is most highly developed in its international aspects; that of the United States in its national aspects. Considering the circumstance that the altering of class relations and institutions generally is the vital feature of Imperialism, the United States shows the typical features of an imperialistic nation. Its reaction against democracy and its imperialistic forms generally are, accordingly, particularly marked and typical in expression.

The early democracy of America, the ideology of Jeffersonian democracy, was the expression of the interests and commodity relations of the small farmers, traders and pioneers. The active flux of life among the people, the free lands out West which irresistibly attracted settlers and its resulting expansion, developed the conditions of social equality and political democracy. These conditions provided the necessary basis for the development of Capitalism, culminating in the great struggle of the Civil War between the system of capital and the system of slavery. In the Civil War the early democracy was immediately victorious, but the conditions produced by its victory swiftly brought its own defeat. The petty bourgeois ideology of democracy of the small traders and independent farmers was crushed under the onward tread of industrial concentration. The expansion westward was no longer independently agrarian, but industrial; it did not produce the conditions of an agrarian democracy, but of an industrial autocracy. The free lands not yet occupied were seized by Capital. The early democracy persisted ideologically and expressed itself in a series of revolts of the farmers and the middle class, but all to no avail: the domination of Capital was unshaken. And this reaction against democracy was emphasized by the appearance of Imperialism; for Imperialism in the United States appears as early as the close of the Civil War, and the construction of the great trans-continental railway systems.

The construction of the Bagdad railway, clearly, was an imperialistic enterprise; it is not so clear that the construction of the trans-continental railway systems of this country was equally an imperialistic enterprise. But it becomes clear when one considers that the purpose of the Bagdad railway was to develop and exploit undeveloped regions; and that was precisely the purpose of the great American railways. The building of a railway in an undeveloped country, generally, is financed in a measure by the government and valuable concessions of lands and mines are secured; and the identical procedure was pursued in this country. The new West played the role of colonies and undeveloped regions, the industrialized East the role of the developed country exporting capital and engaging in financial schemes of development. True enough, there was no mass of unskilled labor in these new regions, as in China and Turkey; but this labor was provided in the shape of immigrants, who were treated with the same brutality as "inferior races" in an undeveloped country. This "internal" Imperialism was in a measure actively promoted by the export of European capital to the United States.

The concentration of industry, based upon this new industrial expansion, proceeded more rapidly and on a larger scale than in any other country, and accelerated the rise of an external American Imperialism, which adventured in Central America and the Carribbeans, and waged an imperialistic war for the "liberation" of Cuba, – and the annexation of the Philippines! The typical conditions of Imperialism developed: the centralization of authority in the national government; intensive brutality toward labor; the appearance of the new forms of progressivism and State Capitalism; the decay of democracy; the altering of class groupings and relations, and the definite cleavage between skilled and unskilled labor, the unions of the aristocracy of labor abandoning the general class struggle and intriguing to become a part of the ruling system of things.

Under these conditions, the attitude of the state toward labor becomes one compounded of cajolery and brutality, and particularly brutality toward the unskilled. In no country in the world, except in a colony, is unskilled labor treated as brutally as in this country. Strikes are crushed ruthlessly by armed force, and even more ruthlessly by the terrorism and tyranny of the courts: strikers are refused the right to picket, are often denied the right of assemblage, their press is suppressed and their representatives thrown into jail, the injunction becomes a Cossack's knout to lash the strikers into subjection. The great industrial revolts of recent years. – Coeur d'Alene, McKees Rocks, Lawrence, Paterson, Ludlow, the Mesaba Range – all these are historic mile-posts in the development of the ruthless policy of suppression adopted by imperialistic State Capitalism against the industrial proletariat of unskilled labor.

The sham democracy of Imperialism is the dominant democracy. The brutality of Imperialism is general. Formerly the carrier of democracy, the nation has become the carrier of Imperialism and reaction. All social groups, except the industrial proletariat of unskilled labor, have become reactionary, are in a status where their interests are promoted by Imperialism, and are counter-revolutionary. The industrial proletariat is determined by its class interests in a struggle against Imperialism and the ruling system of things. Non-proletarian groups can no longer be utilized in the struggle against dominant Capitalism: they are now an integral part of this Capitalism; the proletariat alone can carry on the struggle, independently and through revolutionary Socialism. The struggle for the revival of the old bourgeois democracy cannot in any way become a part of our activity; this activity is determined by the struggle for the new, the fundamental proletarian democracy of communist Socialism.

Footnotes

1. The place of the democratic ideal of equality has been usurped by an oligarchical ideal of domination. But if that ideal seemingly comprises the whole nation in foreign politics, in home politics it changes into an emphasizing of capitalist authority over the working class. The growing power of the workers strengthens at the same time the desire of capital to increase further the power of the state as a security against proletarian demands. Thus the ideology of Imperialism arises and conquers the old liberal ideals. – K. Hilferding, **Das Finanzkapital**.

2. This development it particularly strong and typical in the United States. Its peculiar form of government, and the fact that the Constitution does not specify which department of the government shall assume new functions as they develop – the "twilight zone," which leaves it to circumstances to decide whether the legislature or the executive shall absorb new powers has lodged more and more authority in the Presidency, in the measure that the development of industry imposed new functions upon the government that the Constitution did not provide for. The President has become virtual dictator.

3. The source of the ideology of democracy, with all its traditions and illusions, is the *petite bourgeoisie*. In the second half of the nineteenth century, it suffered a complete internal transformation, but was by no means eliminated from political life. At the very moment that the development of capitalist technique was inexorably undermining its functions, the general suffrage right and universal military service were still giving to the *petite bourgeoisie*, thanks to its numerical strength, an appearance of political importance. Big capital, in so far as it did not completely wipe out this class, subordinated it to its own ends by means of the application of the credit system. All that remained for the political representatives of Big Capital to do was to subjugate the *petite bourgeoisie*, in the political arena, to their purposes, by opening a fictitious credit to the declared theories and prejudices of this class. It is for this reason that, in the decade preceding the war, we witnessed side by side with the gigantic efforts of a reacionary-imperialistic policy, a deceptive flowering of

66

bourgeois democracy with its accompanying reformism and pacifism Capital was making use of the *petite bourgeoisie* for the prosecution of capital's imperialistic purposes by exploiting the ideologic prejudices of the *petite bourgeoisie*. – Leon Trotzky, *Pacifism in the Service of Imperialism*, in **The Class Struggle**, November-December 1917.

4. Under the conditions of Imperialism, progressivism and a liberal ideology become the great means of developing and maintaining the war spirit of a people. The majority Socialism of Germany gives a brutal war a popular and democratic sanction; the imperialistic bourgeoisie of France pursues its sinister purposes through a "people's ministry" consisting of radicals and "Socialists"; the conservative Asquith gives way to the radical Lloyd-George, who seduces labor with liberal slogans, while the Labor Party, through its color of "labor" and its progressivism promotes the war and becomes the last bulwark of defense of British Imperialism.

5. The reformist policy in the most diverse countries aims at an approach toward the progressive and reform-favoring part of the bourgeoisie and in exchange therefor is ready to take part in the administration, to vote budgets, and approve of colonial projects ... Twenty years ago in Germany the liberals and the Catholic Centre party were opponents of militarism and the colonial policy; but since the elections of 1907 all opposition of these petty bourgeois circles against policies of violence and force has disappeared. – Anton Pannekoek, *Imperialism and Social Democracy*, in the **International Socialist Review**, October 1914.

Chapter V
Fundamentals of Socialism

THE class struggle is the dynamic, unifying synthesis of Socialist theory and practice. History is a history of class struggles. A particular class is the carrier of a particular social system; this class is overthrown by a rising class representing a new social system. Society develops in accord with economic conditions; these conditions develop a ruling and a subject class, consequently economic, political and moral antagonisms; the dynamic expression of these antagonisms is their unity in the class struggle. The issues involved in the rivalry of interests is decided by the struggle of class against class, which is not a struggle for particular mercenary interests, but the struggle of social system against social system, the mechanics of social development. The economic development of capitalist society has produced the subject class of the proletariat, providing the material conditions of waging the class struggle for the overthrow of Capitalism, and the proletariat is the carrier of this class struggle.

The proletariat, in the Marxian sense, consists of average or unskilled labor, the form of labor typical of modern Capitalism [1]; it alone is class, as it alone represents the dominant factor in industry and is the carrier of the new social system of communist Socialism; all other classes or social groups are reactionary, decay, disappear, or become absorbed in the general reactionary mass of ruling class interests, in the measure that the process of Big Capital. The antagonisms of interest between labor and capital assume a more general character, and develop into the class struggle of the revolutionary proletariat for the overthrow of Capitalism. This class struggle alone is fundamental; it alone functions dynamically in the process of bringing the Social Revolution and Socialism; and there can be no Socialism that is not firmly based upon the class struggle.

The class struggle implies and makes mandatory the *active, aggressive struggle against Capitalism and for Socialism*; it negates the process of a gradual, pacific penetration of Capitalism by Socialism, a "growing into" the Socialist community. The class struggle and Socialism are made of sterner stuff. All temporary action and achievements are to arouse the independence and virility of the proletariat; the dominant factor is that the proletariat should acquire moral, intellectual and class consciousness, develop its action and class power. The process and means of achievement become of equal importance with the achievement itself. The proletariat must continually express itself in its own class action against Capitalism, and the class struggle becomes more aggressive, more intensive and more general in scope and purposes. And this is the function of Socialism, as the intellectual expression and advance guard of the proletariat, that it absorb, and become itself absorbed in, the class struggle of the proletariat, directing it to the Social Revolution.

In this process, the *consciousness* of the proletariat is the determining consideration. The development of Capitalism, in itself, whether in the form of industrial concentration or the introduction of collectivistic social and political institutions, will not bring Socialism. This development is indispensable as providing the objective, material conditions for Socialism, and important in its influence upon the consciousness of the proletariat. True enough, in its historical aspects, the two developments are phases of one tendency, each equally the product of the conditions of Capitalism. The Socialist movement, however, is directly and particularly concerned with the moral, intellectual and class consciousness of the proletariat, of furthering its aggressive action, and of developing in its ideology and action the concept of the Social Revolution. This subjective development supplements the objective conditions, and it alone can bring Socialism.

The material and dynamic factors in this revolutionary process of the proletarian revolution have been described by

Marx in brilliant and imperishable words [2]:

"As soon as the laborers are turned into proletarians, their means of labor into capital; as soon as the capitalist mode of production stands on its own feet; then the further socialization of labor and further transformation of the land and other means of production also socially exploited and, therefore, common means of production, as well as the further expropriation of private proprietors, take a new form. That which is now to be expropriated is no longer the laborer working for himself, but the capitalist exploiting many laborers. This expropriation is accomplished by the action of the immanent laws of capitalistic production itself, by the centralization of capital. One capitalist always kills many. Hand in hand with this centralization, or this expropriation of many capitalists by few, develop, on an ever extending scale, the co-operative form of the labor process, the conscious technical application of science, the methodical cultivation of the soil, the transformation of the instruments of labor into instruments of labor usable only in common, the economizing of all means of production by their use as the means of production of combined, socialized labor, the entanglement of all peoples in the net of the world-market, and with this, the international character of the capitalistic regime. Along with the constantly diminishing number of the magnates of capital, who usurp and monopolize all advantages of this process of transformation, grows the mass of misery, oppression, slavery, degradation, exploitation [3]; but with this too grows the revolt of the working class, a class always increasing in numbers, and disciplined, united, organized by the very mechanism of the process of capitalist production itself. The monopoly of capital becomes a fetter upon the mode of production, which has sprung up and flourished along with, and under it. Centralization of the means of production and socialization of labor at last reach a point where they become incompatible with their capitalist integument. This integument is burst asunder. The knell of capitalist private property sounds. The expropriators are

71

expropriated ... The transformation of scattered private property, arising from individual labor, into capitalist private property is, naturally, a process incomparably more protracted, violent and difficult than the transformation of capitalistic private property, already practically resting on socialized production, into socialized property. In the former case we had the expropriation of the mass of the people by a few usurpers; in the latter we have the expropriation of a few usurpers by the mass of the people."

There is no indication in this passage, nor anywhere else in Marx, of a Socialist "penetration" of the capitalist system, nor of state and social collectivism as a phase of Socialism in the process of revolutionizing the capitalist order. The material factor of industrial development operates jointly with the dynamic factor of proletarian action. "Centralization of the means of production and socialization of labor at last reach a point where they become incompatible with their capitalist integument. This integument is burst asunder. The expropriators are expropriated" by the proletariat "disciplined, united, organized by the very mechanism of the process of capitalist production itself." It is by and through industry that the proletariat expresses itself, awakens to consciousness of class and power, and acquires the physical and moral reserves for the revolutionary "dictatorship of the proletariat" that will function temporarily as the prelude to the abolition of all class divisions and tyranny, consequent upon the establishment of the full and free democracy of Socialism. All the activity of the proletariat, industrial, political, social, functions for the purpose of developing a partial control of industry that will in the final stage of the revolution i become a complete communistic control of industry by the proletariat, – industrial self-government of the workers.

As capitalist production is internationalized, the class struggle becomes international. The maturity of Socialism is measured by the strength of its ideals of international solidarity *in action*. The nation becomes a fetter upon production, and equally a fetter upon the emancipation of the proletariat. The bourgeoisie breaks the fetters of the nation, through Imperialism, in the interest of its own class purposes, as a national entity; the proletariat must break the fetters of the nation, of national consciousness and action, in the interest of its own local *and* international class purposes. The Social Revolution is an international revolution.

Socialism, accordingly, is exclusively the expression of the interests of the proletariat. Socialism is not the conquest of the state by a political party: it is the conquest of society by the proletariat through industrial and political action. Socialism is not collectivism; it disrupts the collectivism of State Capitalism, which is simply a means of protecting and promoting capitalist interests and more easily oppressing the proletariat, and establishes the communism of industrial self-government.

Socialism is not government ownership or control of industry, two things that are purely a capitalist expression. Socialism struggles for the transformation of the state, not the enlarging of its functions. At first the proletariat is seduced by the idea of state beneficence; it sees in parliamentary struggles and legislation the supreme means of expressing its class interests. As it acquires maturity, the realization is impressed upon its consciousness and action that the state increasingly multiplies the powers for shackling the proletariat; as the facts of its industrial power are recognized, the proletariat becomes contemptuous of the state. Then it appreciates in its action the fundamental concept of Socialism, the class struggle, as expressed in revolutionary Socialism, is a struggle to place the management and control of industry directly in the workers through the overthrow of Capitalism *and* its governmental expression in the state. Socialism, in the words of Engels, is not the government of persons, but the administration of things. The state, and its authority masking itself as democracy, disappears; in its place rises the communism of the initiative centralized in the administrative process of determining the facts of production and distribution, and organizing them in general way for international purposes.

Footnotes

1. In proportion as the bourgeoisie, *i.e.*, capital, is developed, in the same proportion is the proletariat, the modern working class, developed; a class of laborers, who live only so long as they find work, only so long as their labor increases capital. These laborers, who must sell themselves piece-meal, are a commodity, like every other article of commerce, and are consequently exposed to all vicissitudes of competition, to all fluctuations of the market. Owing to the extensive use of machinery and the division of labor, the work of the proletarians has lost all individual character, and, consequently, all charm for the workman. He becomes an appendage of the machine, and it is the most simple, most monotonous, and most easily acquired knack, that is required of him ... The proletariat, the lowest stratum of our present society, cannot stir, cannot raise itself up, without the whole super-incumbent strata of official society being sprung into the air. – **Communist Manifesto.**

2. Karl Marx, **Capital**, Vol.1, chapter XXXII, *Historical Tendency of Capitalist Accumulation.*

3. Many a vulgar bourgeois economist, and here and there a Socialist, has maintained that the "theory of increasing misery" was an essential doctrine of Marxian Socialism. It is not. In the passage quoted above, this is described as a *tendency* of Capitalism, along with another tendency, the *inevitable and growing revolt of the workers.* The increasing poverty of the proletariat is not in any sense a necessary condition for the Social Revolution. Moreover, there is not any sufficiency of material to decide whether poverty is lessening or not; the caste of skilled labor may be more "prosperous," but surely not the mass of unskilled workers. Who will deny, however, that a society which produces such a holocaust as the war, does, even should it better conditions of living, intensify "the mass of misery, oppression, slavery, degradation, exploitation"? On the general problem, L.B. Boudin's **The Theoretical System of Karl Marx** has an interesting passage:

"*Marx does not speak* of the growth of the *poverty* of the working class. The omission of any reference to poverty is very significant in so careful a writer as Marx. This alone would be sufficient warrant for us in assuming that Marx did not consider the growing poverty of the working class a *necessary* result of the evolution of Capitalism ... The lot of the laborer, his general condition as a member of society, must grow worse with the accumulation of capital, *no matter whether his wages are high or low.* His *poverty,* in the ordinary sense of that word, depends upon the amount of wages he gets, but not his *social condition.* And for two reasons. In the first place, because the social condition of any man or class can only be determined by a comparison with the rest of the members or classes of that society. It is not an absolute but a relative quantity. Even the question of poverty is a relative one, and changes from time to time with the change of circumstances. But the question of social condition can never be determined except by a reference to the other classes of society. This is decided not by the absolute amount of worldly goods which they receive in all the worldly goods possessed by society. Thus considered it will be found that the gulf between the capitalist and the working man is constantly growing wider. This is admitted by all as an empirical fact."

Chapter VI
Socialism in Action

THE action of the Socialist movement has been largely the very opposite of its fundamentals. It has theoretically cleaved to these fundamentals, – in Germany most, in the United States least; but it has repeatedly and cumulatively violated them in the actual activity of the movement.

Socialism in action has been making for State Capitalism, not Socialism; it abandoned the proletarian class struggle, and became a general social reform movement; it occupied itself with parliaments and legislation, not with the *action* of the proletariat itself; instead of awakening the revolutionary consciousness of the proletariat, it deadened that consciousness. Socialism became a petty bourgeois Messiah, where it should have been proletarian pioneer and rebel; it has not fulfilled its function of being the intellectual and revolutionary expression of the proletariat.

The revolutionary Socialism of Marx developed into the petty bourgeois Socialism of the Second International. The Paris Commune and its consequent reaction marked the downfall of the First International. The conditions of the ensuing epoch, the. epoch of development along national lines, compelled the proletariat, which, moreover, had not as a whole assumed its typical class character, to lay aside the great task of revolutionizing the world, and to pursue the peaceful development of organization activity. But this organization activity represented only a part of the proletariat; moreover, it came under the influence and domination of petty bourgeois ideals. The organized Socialism that developed out of this state of facts was petty, hesitant, compromising; *and it retained this character after the proletariat emerged into the new revolutionary epoch of Imperialism.*

In becoming a movement of general social reform,

Socialism expressed the interests of the aristocracy of skilled labor and the lower layers of the petty bourgeoisie, and of the new middle class in its earlier stages of development. Practically every revolt, every aspiration of a middle class being destroyed by concentrated industry was echoed in Socialist propaganda and activity. The demand of this class for government ownership of industry became the *leit-motiv* of Socialist propaganda, and Socialism in practice was a movement for government ownership and the extension of the functions of the state generally. Compromise after compromise was struck with the fundamentals of Socialism in order to placate and secure the support of non-revolutionary and non-proletarian groups. The thought of the movement, its activity and representation, became that of the liberal *petite bourgeoisie* and the aristocracy of labor.

The fatal consequence was the betrayal of the new, the real proletariat, which was emerging to consciousness and action, the industrial proletariat of average, unskilled labor. Instead of appreciating the revolutionary potentiality of this class and arousing and expressing its activity, the dominant Socialism betrayed unskilled labor, used it directly and indirectly to promote the petty interests of the aristocracy of Labor and the small bourgeoisie. The revolts of unskilled labor against this reactionary domination were repeatedly crushed, brutally and unscrupulously, by the bureaucracy of organized Socialism. [1] Every intellectual expression of the unskilled in the movement was met with contempt and rejection. It was easier to build a party and a bureaucracy, easier to secure political offices, by catering to non-revolutionary elements; it was a task of real magnitude, and acceptable only to the real revolutionist, to represent and awaken the despised, inchoate mass of the unskilled. But this is precisely the task of Socialism, to express and awaken the real revolutionary class for action and the conquest of power; and in rejecting this task, Socialism became a liberal reform movement, fundamentally non-proletarian and non-revolutionary.

78

Moreover, Socialism adopted the policy of the pacific "penetration" of Socialism into Capitalism, realizing the Socialist community by the extension of capitalist collectivism. The practice of the movement based itself upon the development of Capitalism, instead of upon the revolutionary development of the proletariat. It was a policy that expressed the trend toward State Capitalism and emphasized the trend. Where the Socialist movement was large, as in Germany, it practically absorbed the national liberal forces of social reform; where small, Socialism became an integral part of the national liberal reform movement. Capitalism, not the proletariat, was to bring Socialism, – this was the actual policy of the movement, in spite of utterances and a theoretical system to the contrary.

The task of the proletariat was conceived as decisively the immediate improvement of its material welfare, but this process of improvement was determined almost exclusively by the proposals of skilled labor and the small bourgeoisie. The transformation of Socialist tactics was general; the revolutionary struggle for the overthrow of Capitalism was displaced by the policy of "modifying" Capitalism and softening of class antagonisms. The Socialist theory of Marxism maintained itself, although not in any sense expressing the actual basis of the movement; against it washed the tides of revisionism, which desired an adaptation of theory in accord with the bourgeois practices of the movement, and the tides of revolutionary thought, which desired to have the movement adapt its practice to the requirements of Imperialism and the new revolutionary epoch into which the proletariat had emerged. [2]

The apparent futility of theoretical controversy among the Socialist intellectuals was a consequence of considering differences in tactics as theoretical problems, instead of as essentially problems in practice, in the actual relations of classes and the expression of class interests. The doctrinaire Socialist, the pseudo-Marxist, conceives Socialism as a sort of super-science, unaffected by the conditions which affect bourgeois science. The illusion has an apparently materialistic basis. The doctrinaire Socialist assumes that there are no divisions within the proletariat, its interests being *one*; and that, accordingly, Socialist theory possesses a unity of thought impervious to reactionary influences. But the assumption is not valid. The immediate interests of the working class are *not* one – although they are, ultimately; it *is* split by divisions – between the skilled and the unskilled; and Socialist theory is not only susceptible of reactionary interpretation, but *was used* for reactionary purposes.

Skilled labor was the reactionary factor, aided and abetted by the lower layers of the bourgeoisie – two groups which psychologically approach each other, in the measure that capitalist development raises one and lowers the other. The actual practice of the dominant Socialism produced Revisionism in Germany and Ministerialism in France, the softening of class antagonisms, the open or covert policy of bringing Socialism by the co-operation of classes. It also produced violent tactical differences, in .which pseudo-Marxism actively and consistently discouraged and rejected new revolutionary practices; instead of appreciating the significance of new developments in class relations and tactics, it used these developments to bolster up its pseudo-Marxism, to maintain the *status quo* which allowed the opportunists and moderates to direct the movement straight to disaster. In the hands of these pseudo-Marxists, Marxism was perverted into a reactionary system. In our coming revolutionary struggles, says Anton Pannekoek, Marxism will be our weapon: "Marxism, regarded by the theoreticians of Socialism as the method to explain the past and the present and in their hands degraded into a dry doctrine of mechanical fatalism, again is to come into its birth-right as a theory of revolutionary action." Marx himself said of the pseudo-Marxists: "I sowed dragons' teeth and I reaped fleas."

The acute tactical disputes of Socialism were general. The controversy in the American movement over direct action and political action, IWW and AF of L, was an expression of the conflict between skilled and unskilled, between the proletarian and the petty bourgeois, the early expression of that great upheaval which is coming in American Socialism, and which alone can make Socialism vital and vitalizing. The controversy was complicated by the fact, that the American Socialist Party was peculiarly affected by the conditions of reaction. In Germany, Social-Democracy had a material basis and an ideology of its own, compounded of the liberal aspirations of the Bismarck era and skilled labor, which because of historical conditions lined up with the Social-Democracy. But in this country, and this explains the stunted growth of American Socialism even in its petty opportunist phase, the party had no material basis and ideology of its own. It imported these from Europe. Skilled labor, organized in the AF of L, had determined upon its policy prior to the time it might have been influenced by Socialism, and all attempts of the Socialist Party to "capture" the unions failed miserably: the party adapted itself to the craft unions, but these unions as a whole would have nothing to do with the party. The middle class acted through its own movements, and supported the Socialist party only sporadically and in a small way. The party did not sense the task of expressing the unskilled, of adapting itself to the new conditions which everywhere were developing, and which were largely dominant in the United States. The development of "internal" Imperialism affected the alteration of class groupings and the expression of class interests early and definitely; the party did not appreciate this circumstance; and the Socialist Party became a sort of Mahomet's coffin suspended between heaven and earth. The American party is the most miserable failure of the Second International, measuring its success either in practical or theoretical achievements. It had, and has, all the vices and none of the virtues of the European movement. It is not a representative of the revolutionary proletariat; nor is it honestly even a representative of skilled labor and the small bourgeoisie: it simply *tries* to represent these groups.

Under the petty bourgeois conditions in which it was operating, Socialism became necessarily and essentially a parliamentary movement. The state was the center of Socialist activity. Legislation was conceived as more determinant than action of the proletariat, laws more dynamic than proletarian class power. This activity, naturally, increased the functions and power of the state; the state, under the impetus of Imperialism, intensified its tyranny and brutality against the workers; and the answer to this of Socialist parliamentarians was – more laws, and more power to the state! As governments entered the orbit of Imperialism and State Capitalism, the necessity arose of a struggle against the state through the creative mass action of the proletariat. The necessity was slighted; instead of seeing parliamentarism in its true proportions, parliamentarism became more of a fetish as it became more impotent. Socialism, in fact, was now a part of the government, a prop of the state, a conservative and conserving factor in the ruling system of things. [3]

Having become a national liberal movement of social reform, and a part of the state, Socialism adopted the national ideal and submerged the international. In the measure that the dominant Socialism softened its antagonism to the governing system of things and merged into that system, it drew further away from the militant proletariat and from the Socialism of other nations. There being nothing virik and revolutionary in its policy within the nation, Socialism could not produce a virile and revolutionary international policy. The Socialist movement, operating in an epoch of national development, had become nationalistic, and its nationalistic bias persisted into the new international epoch of Imperialism; it was dominated by the vague democratic nationalism of a preceding era. In the meanwhile, the nation developed into a carrier of Imperialism, discarding democratic nationalism. Socialism went out to fight for the democratic nation, and lo and behold! – Imperialism claimed it for its own, as the nation was now imperialistic. The catastrophe of the Socialist collapse in the crisis of war flowed equally from the circumstance that neither nationally nor internationally had Socialism adapted itself to the conditions and requirements of the era of Imperialism. Socialism had itself become a fetter upon the revolutionary development of the proletariat.

Footnotes

1. In the United States, the unskilled, because of the high degree of "internal" imperialistic development, have acquired a large self-consciousness and activity, and the betrayal of the unskilled by the dominant Socialism and its accessory American Federation of Labor, has nowhere been as complete as in this country. McKees Rocks, Paterson, the Mesaba Range, the great strikes of the unskilled and the IWW generally, have not secured any real support from the dominant forces in the Socialist Party, and have been usually betrayed, either actively or by default. It is true that the party took up the Lawrence strike and the Ludlow outrages, but this was done equally by liberal bourgeois representatives; and in this, again, the Socialist Party was true to its official petty bourgeois ideology.

2. Marxism, originally and essentially a revolutionary system, was perverted by the pseudo-Marxists into an instrument for maintaining the status quo in the Socialist movement, a status becoming increasingly antiquated and consequently reactionary. The struggle between Marxism and Revisionism resulted in a theoretical victory for Marxism; and yet the Social Democracy in practice became increasingly Revisionist, while it was held up by "Marxists" everywhere as the model Socialist Party. These Marxists, typified by Karl Kautsky in Germany, Jules Guesde in France and G. Plekhanov in Russia, were fundamentally a reactionary factor, and each in his particular way collapsed miserably under the test of the war. Their thought expresses the characteristics of bourgeois revolutions, in which, according to Marx, "the phrase surpasses the substance." They represent the "center," the Marxism of which is neither revolutionary nor of Marx, and which, precisely because it uses revolutionary phrases in its criticism of the "right," is particularly dangerous. In a brochure written in April 1917, N. Lenin said:

"The center is the heaven of petty bourgeois phrases, of lip internationalism, of cowardly opportunism, of compromise with the social-patriots. The fact is that the center is not convinced of the necessity of a revolution against the government of its own country; it does not preach that kind of a revolution, it does not wage an incessant fight for the revolution, and it resorts to the lowest, super-Marxist dodges to get out of the difficulty. The members of the center group are routine worshipers, eaten up by the gangrene of legality, corrupted by the parliamentary comedy, bureaucrats accustomed to nice sinecures. Historically and economically they do not represent any special stratum of society; they only represent the transition from the old-fashioned labor movement, such as it was from 1871 to 1914, which rendered inestimable services to the proletariat through its slow, continued, systematic work of organization in a large, very large field, to the new movement which was objectively necessary at the time of the first world-wide war of Imperialism, and which has inaugurated the social revolutionary era."

3. Socialism grew into the state, not the socialist state of the future, but into the capitalistic state of the present. It became a part of this state. It strengthened its own position, but in doing so it strengthened also the state of which it formed a part. It aided the capitalist governments in so developing their powers that they could finally extend their activities beyond their own boundaries. Indirectly, then. Socialism aided in creating the very forces which have brought on the present war. Social Democracy ceased to be an organization of those without a country and became a party of valued citizens whose constructive co-operation was useful to the government and is now especially essential at a time when this government could hardly achieve its purposes without the help of the Socialists. – Heinrich Laufenberg and Fritz Wolfheim, **The Old International and the New**. (This pamphlet was published in 1915, and is an expression of a revolutionary Socialist group in Germany.)

Chapter VII
The Great Collapse

THE test of war during the fatal days of August, 1914, found the dominant Socialism in Europe corrupted by the ideology of national liberal ideals. Democracy and the nation were conceived as synonymous terms: German Socialism declared that Czaristic Russia menaced the democracy of Germany, while the Socialism of Great Britain and France declared that Germany's autocracy menaced the democracy of the world. This ideology of national democracy and the defense of democracy through the nation persisted as a heritage from the days when democratic revolutions were national revolutions, and the nation was the carrier of democracy – of *bourgeois* democracy. But even in these revolutions it was the still immature class of workers that forced the furthest democratic advances; and to-day, under the conditions of Imperialism, the proletarian class struggle alone is the carrier of democracy, of the proletarian democracy which is the only alternative to Imperialism.

An ideology, however, develops out of material conditions and the material conditions of Imperialism produced a new ideology, the ideology of conquest and autocracy. Socialism still clung to the older ideology, in spite of new material conditions; and, moreover, while the phraseology was the same, it had come to mean different things. There was war, the nation was assailed, and it had to be defended as the carrier of democracy, but Imperialism had altered the circumstances and the purposes of the nation. Socialism marched out to fight for the nation, but it was an imperialistic nation and an imperialistic war, the most brutal and shameless war in all history. The voice was the voice of the democratic Jacob, but the hand was the hand of the imperialistic Esau. And, moreover, the dominant Socialism had itself subtly become imperialistic.

It is misleading, however, to maintain that organized

Socialism collapsed upon the declaration of war and its failure to act against the war. Socialism collapsed during the imperialistic epoch of "armed peace" that preceded the war; the collapse in August 1914 was the symbol of a development that marked the transformation of Socialism from a revolutionary and revolutionizing movement into a conservative and conserving factor in the governing system of things. Socialism had collapsed internally, in the national struggle against Capitalism, before it collapsed internationally: the one event followed fatedly and tragically upon the other. Socialism disintegrated as a revolutionary force during the days of peace because it did not carry on the aggressive struggle against imperialistic Capitalism; it disintegrated because it did not adapt itself to the requirements of the menace of war internationally, nor to the altered class relations within the nation. Moreover, organized Socialism could not carry on the aggressive struggle against Imperialism as it was constituted; it had first to transform its material bases and its official theory of State Capitalism; it had to reorganize in accordance with the altered class relations and forms of expression of class interests of Imperialism, adopt a new set of tactics and a new program of purposes determined by the new revolutionary epoch.

The fact is that, prior to the war, organized Socialism *as a social force* had merged into Imperialism, a "liberal" and "pacifist" Imperialism to a certain extent, but Imperialism none the less. The dominant and dominating elements in the Socialist movement – skilled labor, the small bourgeoisie, and the new middle class – had already been seduced by Imperialism. [1] They were not definitely aware of the fact, perhaps, because of an ideology no longer in accord with actual conditions; and this ideology was a mighty contributing factor in the great collapse. Social reform, which was the animating purpose of the movement, had become dependent upon the spoils of Imperialism; the institutions of the nation, in which Socialism was an integral factor, depended, immediately, upon the success of the nation in its imperialistic war. Nationalistic Socialism had a stake in the nation, imperialistic Socialism had a stake in an imperialistic war.

The one militant force which might have been mobilized in the revolutionary struggle, the industrial power of the proletariat of machine labor, which alone may act internationally because of its material conditions, was slightly if at all represented in the councils and proposals of Socialism. Socialism, accordingly, possessed neither the material basis of proletarian power nor the ideology of revolutionary action for the general struggle against Imperialism and war. There was in the Socialist movement no general conception of Imperialism and no real struggle against its menace, except among a small minority of revolutionary Socialists of the left.

The "armed peace" carried the threat of war, and war was the synthetic expression of the general conditions of Imperialism. But in compromising with forces the activity of which generate war, Socialism inevitably compromised with war itself. Its policy against war was a policy of pacifism, which attacks war but allows the class conditions that produce war to persist. The Socialist attack upon militarism, except among minor groups, proceeded within the orbit of pacifism and legality, the pacifism of the small bourgeoisie and its psychological reflex, skilled labor. The compromise with militarism became general: in Germany, attested by voting the war budget in 1913 by the parliamentary Social Democracy under the cowardly and characteristically petty bourgeois pretext of "equalizing" taxation; in France and the International generally, by not emphasizing the campaign against Imperialism and militarism, or adopting the policy of pacifism in the campaign.

The policy on war and militarism of the dominant Socialism was as petty bourgeois as its policy on other major problems.

Instead of a revolutionary attack upon Imperialism and militarism and preparations to prevent war or convert it into a civil war of the oppressed against the oppressors, and for Socialism, there was scheme after scheme proposed to *evade* war. The theory of Socialism made it visualize clearly the menace of war; its practice and animating purposes prevented it from offering any real opposition to the coming of war, and none to war itself. Socialism had an abiding horror of war – but sentiments are not a substitute for deeds; and this horror expressed itself while simultaneously pursuing a policy that promoted the coming of war. This horror of war the dominant Socialism shared with the *petite bourgeoisie* generally; but this bourgeoisie allied itself with an Imperialism that inexorably produced war. Capitalism itself, as a whole, may be said to have a horror of war: it is risky; but still it pursues a policy that makes for war, – a state of things particularly apparent in France. [2] The Dominant Socialism accepted the softening of class antagonisms through collectivism as a means of "growing into" Socialism; and it accepted pacifism and its policy of gradually softening and regulating national antagonisms as the means to general peace. One policy is related to the other, and each is the consequence of relinquishing the general revolutionary struggle against Capitalism, of the perversion of revolutionary Socialism ... And through the years comes the bitter sarcasm of Marx, "I sowed dragons' teeth and I reaped fleas."

It was a national set of circumstances that dictated this policy of the dominant Socialism; and Socialism clung to its nationalistic bias at a time when Capitalism was internationalizing itself through Imperialism. The coming of war and war itself can be effectively fought only by subordinating the national ideal to the international. This Socialism did not accomplish. At each international congress proposals for *international action* against war met disaster on the rocks of the national ideology dominating every Socialist party, – an ideology, moreover, which equally prevented national action against war. Imperialism negated nationalism, while using it in its service; Socialism emphasized nationalism.

88

The result inevitably was disaster, a catastrophic collapse.

Under these conditions, Socialism might talk against impending war, but it could not act. In the tragic ten days of July it did talk, furiously, flamboyantly, smugly, but it never acted; *it never considered action*, satisfying itself with the pacifist activity of demonstration and denunciation.

The salient feature of the activity of dominant Socialism during these ten days was a dependence upon forces *outside* itself to prevent the coming of war. The Socialists denounced war; they held demonstrations; they threatened the governments; they did everything, in short, except that which might have produced results: *definite, determined action based upon the class struggle and the revolutionary activity of the proletariat itself.*

If the dominant Socialism had been revolutionary, it would have issued a declaration of distrust in all governments, actively and aggressively opposed the coming of war *by deeds*, and prepared for civil war in the event of a declaration of war. Action of this, character might have prevented war – a government would hesitate to engage in war without the support of the working class. But even if it did not prevent war, it would, at least, have been a gesture worthy of the revolutionary aspirations of Socialism; moreover, and still more important, it would have given Socialism and the proletariat a strategic and tactical advantage over the governments during the war, hastened the coming of peace and determined the conditions of peace; and, considering the Russian Revolution and the crisis precipitated by the revolutionary dictatorship of the proletariat in Russia, it would have meant international action for the Social Revolution in Europe. But the dependence upon everything except the mass action of the proletariat, was fatal. Socialism was demoralized, corrupted, palsied except for evil, and the proletariat was curbed in its potential action.

The task of organizing action against an impending war

in the form of an international General Strike was left to the discretion of the International Socialist Bureau by the Stuttgart Congress in 1907. The Bureau, meeting July 20, 1914, at Brussels, adopted a resolution of which two paragraphs are significant:

"The Bureau considers it an obligation for the workers of all nations concerned not only to continue but even to strengthen their demonstrations against war in favor of peace, and a settlement of the Austro-Servian conflict by arbitration.

"The German and French workers will bring to bear on their governments the most vigorous pressure in order that Germany may secure in Austria a moderating action, and in order that France may obtain from Russia an undertaking that she will not engage in the conflict. On their sides the workers of Great Britain and Italy shall sustain these efforts with all the power at their command."

The only indication of the General Strike in the activity of the Bureau was in a resolution "congratulating" the workers of Russia "on their revolutionary attitude" [a big General Strike was on in Russia] and inviting them "to continue their heroic efforts against Czarism as one of the most effective guarantees against the threatened world war." But if a General Strike in Russia, not directed primarily against the war and affecting only some hundreds of thousands of workers, was "one of the most effective guarantees against the threatened world war," why did not the Bureau try to multiply this effectiveness by issuing a call for similar strikes in Germany and France *against the war*? It is clear why this was not done, because the dominant Socialism was *not against the war in a revolutionary sense*, if actually at all; it was against the war only in the sense of bourgeois pacifism, with the gangrene of a national ideology eating away at its vitals. Moreover, there was already talk of the defense of democracy and the nation, talk of this or that nation, always never one's own nation, being the aggressor; there was no international unity during the crisis because there had not been

90

any during the period proceeding. [3]

The dominant spirit at the great anti-war demonstration in Brussels, July 29, was one of impotent threatening and confidence in one's own government. Emile Vandervelde spoke; so did Jean Jaurès and Hugo Haase. Haase held up the spectre of revolution – as if, not being backed up by definite, organized, aggressive action, it could frighten the governments; and the threat was still further invalidated by Haase's statement that the German government was working for peace! Jaurès said that the French government, in co-operation with the "admirable" English government, was pursuing a policy of peace.

This was an attitude fraught with danger. The policy of peace a bourgeois government may pursue is circumscribed within the definite limits of ruling class interests; moreover, Jaurès' and Haase's attitude converted the possibility of proletarian acquiescence in the war into a certainty by developing confidence in the governments, which under all circumstances should be distrusted. France desired peace, but yet it was clear she would stand by Russia in the event of war; the imperialistic stakes were too immense. In this emergency, revolutionary Socialist action was indispensable and alone consistent, – unambiguous formulation of a policy directed against governments through strikes and general mass action. The good intentions of governments are as a reed, – and the revolutionist, of all people, should know it. The Social Democracy of Germany not only did not organize resistance against the government and the coming of war, but was already preparing to participate in the war: this was the hideous fact underneath all the grandiloquent phrases. The Berlin **Vorwärts**, in the early days, made more than one threat of revolution, and it tore to shreds the claim of a war of democracy against Czarism. But its editorial of July 28 concluded: "They [the peoples of Europe] demand from their governments intervention against this political madness. They demand unambiguous representations in Vienna, in Berlin, in St. Petersburg." On August 1 the **Vorwärts** pleaded that "there is still time for negotiations." But war was declared, and then came Socialist acquiescence in the infamy of an accomplished fact.

The policy and action described are typical of bourgeois pacifism generally – first denunciation and threats hurled at the government, then pleadings addressed to that same government, and then acquiescence in and acceptance of the acts of the governments. [4]

All through the crisis *action* was never proposed or pursued by the dominant Socialism; action was left to the governments. The governments acted for war; and then Socialism equally acted for war and justified the war, mobilized the masses for the war, thereby completely crushing the possibility of proletarian action, – except among minor groups and the intrepid Socialist Party of Italy.

The indictment against the dominant Socialism does not depend upon its failure to prevent the war: Socialism might not prevent a war, and still retain its integrity and revolutionary honor, prepared to act on the basis of the class struggle at the earliest opportunity. The American representatives of opportunist Socialism, together with their recognized leader, Morris Hillquit, argue that there was no collapse of the International because Socialism *could not* prevent the war. Admitting the premises, in spite of the fact that the dominant Socialism did not really try to prevent war, was not the general justification of the war by the dominant Socialism, and manufacturing its ideology, a collapse of the International? The stain upon the dominant Socialism of Europe, particularly of Germany and Austria, is that it used all its efforts to make an imperialistic war popular with the workers; it adopted the arguments of the imperialistic governments; it consciously mobilized the proletariat for slaughter in an imperialistic war. *This* is the real collapse, and the sophistry and hypocrisy, the dishonest "explanations" of the moderate Socialist explain nothing, except their own petty bourgeois ideals and revolutionary cowardice.

During the war, the dominant Socialism struck a truce with the ruling class *"burgfrieden"* in Germany, the *"union sacré"* in France. Socialism "suspended" the class struggle, relinquishing the final measure of its independence, and developed into an agency of the governments, acting with the turpitude of a moral pervert and the insolence of a gutter strumpet. The proletariat was offered as a sacrifice upon the altar of Mars by the very movement that previously offered it emancipation. The dominant Socialism manufactured an ideology for the war more subtle, more dangerous; more calculated to betray the proletariat to its class enemy, than all the acts and propaganda of the governments.

The official majority Socialists of Germany, directed by the infamous Scheidemann, became the confidantes of the government and its *comis voyageurs*: they went to Belgium to "explain" to the Socialists that Germany could not have acted otherwise than by violating Belgium; they went to Italy to seduce the Socialist Party to advocate Italy's entrance into the war on the side of Germany, but were contemptuously rejected and bastinadoed. Jules Guesde – yes, the revolutionary Jules Guesde of yesteryear – urged Italy to war in the cause of democracy; and Guesde, Albert Thomas and the majority in the French party developed into uncompromising adherents of "war to the finish," come what might. The Socialist majority became an active force in suppressing potential proletarian revolt; it generally acquiesced in the most brutal acts of the governments. When the German proletariat prepared great strikes and demonstrations for May Day 1917, the **Vorwärts** carried on a propaganda against the plans, aided and abetted by the party bureaucracy. Civil peace was maintained by Socialism, in spite of the fact that Capitalism repeatedly violated the peace in its own sinister interests. The Russian Revolution, particularly when it definitely developed into a proletarian revolution, sent a thrill of energy and enthusiasm through the proletariat of Europe, but it could not immediately break the shackles imposed upon it by the dominant Socialism, which used all its power to prevent a revolutionary uprising. The French parliamentary Socialists answered the call to action of the revolutionary proletariat of Russia by the petty bourgeois appeal for the Revolution to align itself with the Allies, – in the words of Guesde – "first victory, and then the republic." The great strikes and demonstrations of January and February 1918 in Austria and Germany, were broken by the antagonism of the dominant Socialism and the imperialistic regular unions of skilled labor; while the **Vorwärts** declared that it didn't want a revolution, but simply that the government should "mediate" the differences between it and the proletariat.

During the war, dominant Socialism acted as the governments acted; a *volte face* on the part of the governments usually produced the same result among the representatives of the *petit-bourgeois* Socialists, who indulged in contemptible intrigues in the interest of their particular imperialistic government. The attempt to convene a Socialist Congress for peace at Stockholm in 1917 was vitiated by the dominant Socialism of the Allies and turned into a miserable pro-German intrigue by the cohorts of Scheidemann and Victor Adler. The dominant Socialism entered the active service of Imperialism, becoming its most valued ally where it should have been its worst enemy.

The class struggle is fundamental. Divested of jhe class struggle, Socialism becomes either utopia or reaction. But events are instinct with a fatal logic: the process of softening class antagonisms and divisions during peace inevitably generates the complete abandonment of the class struggle during war. The cycle of collapse is completed. It is during war that the class struggle should reach its maximum intensity: all the conditions of multiplied oppression and exploitation are a call to carry on the class struggle. War does not change the issue, but emphasizes it: the class struggle against Capitalism. [5]

Each and every abandonment of the class struggle is a

step *away* from Socialism. The nation has become imperialistic. In the course of the war, accordingly, the national democratic ideology was transformed by large groups within the Socialist movement, who projected an imperialistic ideology and accepted Imperialism as a necessary stage to Socialism. Heinrich Cunow, one of the intellectual leaders of the German Social Democracy, is characteristic of these groups in his theoretical defense of Imperialism. Cunow maintains that there will be no immediate collapse of Capitalism and no early victory of Socialism; that illusions arising out of this belief are responsible for Socialist disappointment caused by the war. Cunow counsels a closer scrutiny of the actual course of development, and proceeds to a defense of Imperialism:

"The new imperialistic phase of development is just as necessarily a result of the innermost conditions of the financial existence of the capitalist class, is just as necessary a transitional stage to Socialism, as the previous stages of development, for example, the building up of large scale industry ... The demand, 'we must not allow Imperialism to rule, we must uproot it,' is just as foolish as if we had said at the beginning of machine industry: 'no machine must be tolerated, let us destroy them, and let us henceforth allow only hand-work.'"

Cunow's conclusion is legitimate in the light of the petty bourgeois, reformist activity of the Social Democracy. The struggle against Imperialism is futile *if it is limited within the orbit of Capitalism.* But Imperialism is the climax of the development of Capitalism; it means Capitalism, fully developed, trying to break through the national ideology and national frontiers in a desperate effort to maintain its ascendancy by conquering new fields of expansion; and it means, accordingly, Capitalism initiating an epoch in which the Social Revolution becomes a necessity and a fact. The struggle against Imperialism must consist of the revolutionary struggle of the class conscious proletariat for the Social Revolution. Imperialism is a menace: it is a menace to the old system of

95

Capitalism and it is a menace to the oncoming system of communist Socialism. Imperialism is the desperate attempt of Capitalism to maintain its supremacy, and it sets the world afire in the desperation of its struggles. Capitalism is revolting against the fetters imposed by its own contradictions, through Imperialism; the proletariat must respond by the class struggle against Capitalism and Imperialism, by the Social Revolution. But this conclusion and necessity, clearly, imply a struggle of the oncoming proletarian revolution against the dominant Socialism. The petty bourgeois, reformistic Socialism rejects the struggle against Imperialism and collapses tactically because it is itself a part of the imperialistic epoch; it, accordingly, accepts Imperialism as a necessary stage to Socialism, meanwhile clownishly crying that it is all in accord with revolutionary Marxism, that the inevitable collapse of Capitalism is coming, anyhow: "God's in his heaven, all's right with the world." The sins of Imperialism are washed clean in the holy water of pseudo-Marxian theory.

The spirit of Cunow's analysis, moreover, expresses a dangerous tendency latent in pseudo-Marxian thought, and which contributed intellectually to the great collapse. It is what may be termed the "historical imagination," the tendency to view contemporary phenomena as one views the phenomena of history, in scholarly retrospection. This necessarily leads to reactionary concepts and paralysis of action. If there is error in the judgment of history, however much more might there not be in judging history in the making? Even in history only the large, general developments can be considered inevitable, – the broad tendencies of social evolution. One may speak of the "inevitable" this and the "inevitable" that after the event, perhaps; but it is dangerous to do so before the event. And particularly if we possess an insight into the processes of history; for of what practical value is this insight if it is not used in an *attempt*, at the very least, to direct the course of history?

Cunow sees in Imperialism a "necessary transitional stage to Socialism." The dominant Social Democracy of

Germany seems to possess real genius for discovering "transitional stages" to Socialism, and for emphasizing any and all things except the revolutionary development and activity of the proletariat itself. A generation ago, the conquest of political democracy was considered a "necessary transitional stage" to Socialism, and ended in making the Social Democracy a party of bourgeois democracy and social reform. Now the German Socialist majority seems to have forgotten this particular "transitional stage" and allies itself with a very opposite tendency, Imperialism, the arch-enemy of democracy. [6] The prattle of 'transitional stages" is simply a palliation of the refusal to engage in the revolutionary struggle. The imperialistic German government decides upon a certain political course, and then calls upon the historian and the philosopher to manufacture the intellectual justification; the German Social Democracy decides to adopt a non-Socialist policy, and then calls upon the pseudo-Marxist to harmonize it with the robust, revolutionary philosophy of Marx.

Imperialism is a necessary stage, and will become a permanent stage of Capitalism, *if the Social Revolution is not considered.* And the fight against Imperialism is a dynamic means of bringing the Social Revolution. Should Socialists cease their opposition to the exploitation of labor because that exploitation is necessarily a result of Capitalism? Is Socialism to become the historian, analyzing the developments of Capitalism, instead of a revolutionary and revolutionizing factor in these developments? Is the Socialist movement to renounce its revolutionary heritage for the flesh-pots of Imperialism? In fighting Imperialism Socialism doubly fights Capitalism; in abandoning the fight against Imperialism it simultaneously and necessarily abandons the fight against Capitalism. For Imperialism is nothing but an acute expression of Capitalism, a symptom that it is rotten-ripe for change. The development of machine industry was an expression of Capitalism in its initial stage; Imperialism is an expression of the final stage of Capitalism, which to-day is over-developed. Capitalism seeks through Imperialism a means of avoiding an industrial and social collapse. The maturity of industrial development poses the problem – either Imperialism or Socialism. Cunow is wrong, there *is* an alternative to Imperialism, and that is Socialism, while there was none to machine industry. The answer of Capitalism to the impending collapse is Imperialism and war; the answer of Socialism can only be and must be the Social Revolution.

As the war developed, there was a slight recovery among the representatives of the center, typified by the majority at the Zimmerwald Conference, and which in Germany led to the formation of the Independent Socialist Party. The animating spirit of this party, however, was the old pseudo-Marxism which had justified the conservatism of the movement; it still expressed the facts of the labor and Socialist movement prior to the war, the old tactics, the old policy, not the new requirements of a revolutionary epoch. The new party reverted to the psychology of the past; it did not completely sever the strings that bound it to petty bourgeois, reformistic Socialism. The Independent Socialist Party waged a contemptible campaign against the Bolsheviki. Hugo Haase declared that it was legitimate to vote against the war credits, – because there was not a foreign soldier on German soil, thereby emphasizing the determination of the French Socialists to support their government, as German soldiers were on *their* soil.

The intellectual genius of the new party was Karl Kautsky, the vacillator, the harmonizer, the man who manufactured one theoretical justification after another for the abandonment of Socialism by the Social Democracy, the man who shortly after the war broke formulated the monstrous doctrines that the International was an instrument during peace, but not during war, and that all Socialists were justified in supporting their governments as under the conditions of Imperialism all nations were on the defensive. The Independent Socialist Party, as constituted, is a force for re-establishing the *status quo ante*, – a calamity that revolutionary Socialism must fight against with might and main. These representatives of the center did not issue a call to revolutionary action, they did not measure up to the requirements of a great historic crisis. The old phrases, the old policy, the old tactics: is it with these that we shall revolutionize the world? The dead must bury their dead. The bulk of the revolutionary Socialists of Germany, including Karl Liebnecht, Franz Mehring, Rosa Luxemburg and Karl Radek, uncompromisingly attacked the new party, organizing independently, in the "Spartacus'" group and the group "Internationale." The day of compromise is past forever: Socialism must completely re-constitute itself as an uncompromising revolutionary force in accord with the tactical necessity of the new epoch.

The old Social Democracy, captained by Scheidemann, retained possession of the machinery and press of the party, and became more completely identified with the capitalist state, more completely an integral part of the existing system of things. It made no bones of the matter, either. Unblushingly, insolently, it placed its faith in the might of the German nation, used all its energy for a victory of its national Imperialism. The emancipation of the proletariat, the Russian Revolution, the future of the world, were all meaningless to the Social Democracy, all simply instruments for promoting its bourgeois purposes by means of a brutal Imperialism. The existing system was accepted as the only conceivable basis upon which to work; this system should be modified, perhaps; but revolutionized – never! The state, the imperialistic state of Capitalism, was the centre of all activity, and the action of the Social Democracy was to be determined by the state. Socialism, according to the new dispensation, was no longer a class movement of the proletariat: it was a movement of all the classes, through the co-operation of which alone could Socialism be established. It was precisely this program and policy that the British Labor Party gradually developed under the pressure of war, and which it clearly formulated in January 1918. The Labor Party also accepted the war, and promoted the war by mobilizing the masses through the slogan of democracy; it became a part of the state, the main-stay of British hopes of victory; it constituted itself a party of all the classes by opening its doors to "workers of the brain."

The Social Democracy was now definitely and completely a party of "laborism" and the small bourgeoisie, a counter-revolutionary partry over whose prostrate corpse alone the proletariat could march to victory. [7]

The Socialist-imperialist and social-patriot generally base their conception of "Socialism" upon the development of Capitalism in itself; the revolutionary Socialist bases it upon the class development of the proletariat. Capitalism is fully developed; the proletariat must develop the revolutionary consciousness and action for its historic mission of overthrowing class rule. Socialism cannot "grow into" Capitalism through collectivism and the co-operation of classes; Socialism must overthrow Capitalism. Instead of being softened, class antagonisms and the class struggle must be emphasized; instead of compromise with Capitalism, relentless attack upon the whole capitalist regime as determined by the conditions of Imperialism.

The issue posed by the great collapse is this: Shall Socialism organize dynamically for the overthrow of Capitalism, or shall it organize for the perpetuation of Capitalism through a policy of national social-Imperialism and State Capitalism?

Footnotes

1. The social-patriots are Socialists in words and patriots in fact, who agree to defend their fatherland in an imperialistic war, and particularly this imperialistic war. These men are our class-enemies. They have gone over to the bourgeois camp. They count among their numbers the majority of Social Democrats in every nation ... The social-patriots are the enemies of our class, they are bourgeois in the midst of the labor movement. They represent layers or groups of the

working class which have been practically bought by the bourgeoisie, through better wages, positions of honor, etc., and which help their bourgeoisie to exploit and oppress smaller and weaker nations, and to take part in the division of capitalistic spoils. – N. Lenin, **Task of the Proletariat in Our Revolution**, Petrograd, September 1917.

2. The *petit bourgeois* sends to parliament a radical who has promised him to preserve peace ... This radical-"pacifistic" *bloc* of deputies gives birth to a radical ministry, which at once finds itself bound hand and foot by all the diplomatic and military obligations and financial interests of the French *bourse* in Russia, Africa and Asia. Never ceasing to pronounce the proper pacifistic sentences, the ministry and parliament automatically continue to carry on a world-policy which involves France in war. – Leon Trotsky, *Pacifism in the Service of Imperialism*, in **The Class Struggle** of November-December 1917.

3. The question *how* the war could be resisted was never even raised, because the question *whether* the war ought to be resisted was not even answered with a decisive Yes. – Anton Pannekoek, *Imperialism and Social Democracy*, **International Socialist Review**, October 1914.

4. In spite of its declaration against the war, the American Socialist party has pursued a similar policy – the ideas of its dominant personnel are identical with the social-pacifists and social-patriots in the European movement. The resolutions and declarations of the National Executive Committee since August 1914 are instinct with the spirit of bourgeois pacifism. The party bureaucracy allied itself with the "radical" pacifists, abandoned the class struggle, and confused the whole issue of war and peace. The Resolution against war adopted at the St. Louis Convention is largely contradictory and insincere: it means all things to all men. To be sure, the radical part of the delegates forced certain revolutionary declarations into the Resolution; but these have been repeatedly violated and abandoned by the party bureaucracy. Morris Hillquit, under pressure, accepted these declarations; and after the Convention proceeded to explain them away. The climax of his opportunist policy was his answer to the question put to him by William Hard whether, if he had been a member of Congress, he would have voted in favor of war. Hillquit answered (**New Republic**, December 1, 1917, reprinted in the **New York Call** of December 5): "If I had believed that our participation would shorten the world-war and force a better, more democratic and

more durable peace, I should have favored the measure, regardless of the cost and sacrifices of America. My opposition to our entry into the war was based upon the conviction that it would prolong the disastrous conflict without compensating gains to humanity," That's all! – a complete abandonment and repudiation of the St. Louis Resolution, a policy of the worst bourgeois pacifism. Moreover, the officials of the party, and through them the party, became allied with the People's Council, a typical product of bourgeois pacifism. The People's Council, and through it the official bureaucracy of the Socialist Party, destroyed the peace movement, *mobilized the ideology of the masses for the war* by declaring President Wilson had adopted *its* terms of peace. Meyer London, the party's representative in Congress, admirably performed the function of a lackey of Imperialism disguised by a bland hypocrisy of words and deeds. When the proletarian revolution in Russia swept into power, the party officially was silent, while the New York Call confessed an ignorance bordering on intellectual bankruptcy and an infamous palliation of its petty bourgeois soul. The party was silent on the Russian proposal for an armistice; it was silent on the peace policy of the proletarian revolution, and after President Wilson spoke nice words about the Russians, the National Executive Committee adopted a resolution presumably in line with the policy of revolutionary Russia, but actually nothing of the sort. Moreover, the official leaders of the party openly or covertly justify the policy of majority Socialism in Europe; and they will after the war in all probability agree with Scheidemann, Thomas & Co., on the theory that the social-patriots engaged in a "defensive" war. The party membership on the whole revealed a fine integrity and instinctive class consciousness, but it was baffled by the party bureaucracy, which divided into adherents of the war and adherents of a policy of conciliation and pacifism.

5. To the great historic appeal of the **Communist Manifesto** is added an important amendment and it reads now, according to this revision : "Workers of the world unite in peace and cut one another's throats in war!" Today, "Down with the Russians and French!" – tomorrow, "We are brothers all!" This convenient theory introduces an entirely novel revision of the economic interpretation of history. Proletarian tactics before the outbreak of war and after must be based on exactly opposite principles. This pre-supposes that social conditions, the bases of our tactics, are fundamentally different in war from what they are in peace. According to the economic interpretation of history

as Marx established it, all history is the history of class struggles. According to the new revision, we must add : except in times of war. Now human development has been periodically marked by wars. Therefore, according to this new theory [advocated by Karl Kautsky, the harmonizer *par excellence* of bourgeois Socialist practices with pseudo-Marxian theory] social development has gone on according to the following formula: a period of class struggles, marked by class solidarity and conflicts within the nations; then a period of national solidarity and international conflicts – and so on indefinitely. Periodically the foundations of social life as they exist during peace change in time of war. And again, at the moment of the signing of a treaty of peace, they are restored. This is not, evidently, progress by means of successive "catastrophes;" it is rather progress by means of a series of somersaults. Society develops, we are to suppose, like an iceberg floating down a warm current; its lower portion is melted away, it turns over, and continues this process indefinitely. Now all the known facts of human history run straight counter to this new theory. They show that there is a necessary and dialectic relation between the class struggle and war. The class struggle develops into war and war develops into the class struggle; and thus their essential unity is proved. It was so in the medieval cities, in the wars of the Reformation, in the Flemish wars of liberation, in the French Revolution, in the American Rebellion, in the Paris Commune, and in the Russian uprising in 1905. [And in Russia, again in 1917.] – Rosa Luxemburg, *The Class Struggle During War*, in **The International** (1915), a magazine started by Rosa Luxemburg and Franz Mehring, and suppressed by the German government after the appearance of the first issue. (Reprinted in **The New International** of May 5, 1917.)

6. The cross-currents of Socialist thought are not developed clearly in the American movement, because of its historical conditions. But they exist, if only in latent form. John Spargo, William English Walling, and others, including their Social Democratic League, adopted completely the standpoint of the most reactionary social-patriots of Europe. Ernest Untermann, in a series of articles in the **Milwaukee Leader** during 1915, accepted and applied Cunow's position. In the course of his arguments, Untermann uses a phrase, "Revolution by Reaction," which, caricature as it is and because it is caricature, aptly characterizes the Socialist-imperialist's attitude. "Militarism," says Untermann, "and colonial Imperialism today seem the worst enemies of Democracy and Socialism, yet no other power so rapidly and

effectively enforces co-operative discipline, kills anarchist individualism, destroys petty business enterprise and undermines the whole capitalist system nationally and internationally so thoroughly as these arch-enemies of the common good are doing." According to Untermann, "Our American imperialists, like their European brethren, must work for the revolution, whether they like it or not," and he favored the conquest of Mexico, as it is a "perfervid illusion" to hope that "American intervention can and must be prevented:" "Now the alternative facing the American capitalists is: either a constitutional government of Mexicans controlled by influences hostile to American capitalists, or annexation of Mexico. If they choose annexation, they will give to the Mexicans with one hand what they take with the other. For if Mexico is annexed, the Mexican people lose their national independence, but they gain – admission to the American labor movement and the American Socialist Party." Wonderful gains – considering the reactionary character of the American labor movement and Socialist Party, united against the unskilled workers and favoring anti-immigration. Untermann's views are substantially the views of Victor L. Berger, who advocated editorially in the **Leader** the conquest of Mexico, and who is a social-imperialist and social-patriot of the worst type. Moreover, it must be borne in mind that the policy of the American Socialist majority during peace is identical with, if a caricature of, the policy pursued by the European Socialist majority.

7. The Würzburg Congress of the Social Democracy, in the second half of 1917, formulated the new policy of the party. The delegates were in complete accord with the government and a policy of social-imperialism; the general sentiment was that it is about time to put an end to "cloister science," and that the new program should be puri6ed of the "Marxist scholastic." Scheidemann ushered in the new dispensation with a speech characteristic of the social-imperialist policy. Among other things, he said:

"With regard to tactics we have become more flexible; because, owing to the war, the worker's position has considerably changed. Imperialism was forced to fight its battles in this war with the proletariat. And yet the war has not succeeded in strengthening the class rule of the bourgeoisie over the masses; but on the contrary the workers have everywhere learned that the state for which they fight will after the war be less than ever a mere class enemy. The working class is not any more an amorphous mass. It is an organized body. And there are a thousand reasons why the organized workers cannot oppose themselves to the state. This they have nowhere done. If organized labor fought the battles for the existence of the state it did not in the least intend to be a mere cannon fodder, and everywhere it held high its particular ideals and class objects. The proletariat is not a mercenary soldier of the ruling classes but an ally who came out of the need of the moment, who at the end, however, will present his bill."

And this is what becomes of the historic mission of the proletariat to overthrow Capitalism – that it consciously ally itself with the bourgeoisie and march out, for the purpose of "presenting its bill," to rape Belgium, devastate France, and crush the Russian Revolution! "The most interesting point in Scheidemann's speech," said the Berlin **Vorwärts**, "was the statement that the socialization of society can not be brought about through the exclusive efforts of Social Democracy. The solution of this great task awaits the aid of all other parties." Oh, yes – yes, indeed. And the first step toward this peculiar Socialism, of course, is to destroy Serbia, subjugate Austria, rape Belgium, devastate France, crush the Russian Revolution, justify and promote the most brutal purposes of Imperialism, – and, incidentally, crush the on-coming proletarian revolution in Germany.

Chapter VIII
Socialist Readjustment

I

THE process of Socialist readjustment depends, immediately and ultimately, upon readjustment within the nation; it must start with the reconstruction of the material basis of the movement and the adoption of revolutionary purposes and tactics in the national struggle against the ruling class. This internal readjustment will necessarily express itself in the readjustment of the Socialist International, the creation of a New International that will not break down when the call comes for international revolutionary action, as its constituent national groups will have adopted revolutionary tactics in the internal struggle against imperialistic Capitalism. The attempt to reorganize the International of Socialism without transforming its constituent national groups will inevitably mean a new collapse, new and more acute disappointments. Socialism collapsed internationally because it had previously collapsed nationally; revolutionary action within the nation alone can impose revolutionary action upon the International of the proletariat. It is a general process of reconstruction: the one promotes the other.

The struggle against Imperialism is the starting point of this readjustment, the factor determining our new immediate purposes and tactics, which must break with the immediate purposes and tactics of the past. Under the conditions of the new era, Socialism either organizes aggressively against Imperialism and for the overthrow of the capitalist regime, or it becomes completely submerged in social-Imperialism and reaction.

The new conditions require an abandonment of the fallacy of "growing into" Socialism, and the acceptance of the fact that revolutionary struggle alone is the determinant factor in Socialist policy. The revolution becomes, not an aspiration of the future, but an inspiration instinct in the immediate action of the proletariat. The proletariat is a supremely utilitarian class, dominated by the sense of reality; and through this reality of actual struggle the revolutionary spirit has to express itself. The self consciousness of the mass is the impulse of the struggle, the reality of its life and material conditions the fulcrum by which it is moved to revolutionary action. The proletarian mass is animated by the enthusiasm of struggle, rather than by the ideal; but out of this struggle arises the ideal, for the conditions of its activity impose a revolutionary expression. Struggle succeeds struggle, becoming more general, more centralized and national in scope, and project an international struggle by the propulsion of the activity itself. International action becomes imperative. The dualism in Socialist tactics disappears there is no political action alone, there is no industrial action alone, but one unified action : the acceptance and merging of all means into the general revolutionary action of the proletariat. The class struggle becomes more conscious, more bitter and uncompromising, more revolutionary in scope, means and aspirations. Capitalism meets attack after attack, weakening in the measure that the proletariat acquires the consciousness and strength developing out of its struggles. Capitalism succumbs not to an ultimate. Revolutionary acTalbne, but to a series of revolutionary acts which inevitably result in the Social Revolution. "The bourgeoisie, born in the Revolution, maintaining itself in a struggle against the Revolution, can only be overcome by the Revolution." [1]

The general process of Socialist readjustment is not determined by the formulation of theoretical problems; it is not a study in theory, but a study in the practice and the material basis of the Socialist movement. There is no Socialism without the class struggle, and the carrier of this class struggle is the agency through which Socialism functions. The readjustment of Socialism, accordingly, is determined by adjusting itself to that class in society which is the most typical product of modern industry, and consequently revolutionary. Socialism must locate this class, and express its material conditions of struggle and development.

Socialism reorganizes in accordance with the altered class relations and expression of class interests of imperialistic Capitalism, which for the first time approximate the conditions considered essential for the Social Revolution by the founders of Socialism.

II

According to our analysis, Socialism has been dominated by the interests of skilled labor, marshaled by the petty bourgeoisie and the intellectuals of the new middle class. This domination directed the movement straight to disaster.

It should not require much discussion to prove the reactionary character of the remnants of the small bourgeoisie and representatives of the new middle class. The *petite bourgeoisie* is not only not a revolutionary class, it is a class beaten in the struggle for social supremacy, destroyed as an independent factor and a vassal of dominant Capitalism, a class that complains but dares not revolt. Its interest in Socialism, except in the case of isolated individuals, who rise superior to their petty class interests, is simply to use the prestige of Socialism to promote its own narrow interests. The small bourgeoisie is not even any longer reactionary in the sense of Marx, that "it tries to roll back the wheels of history"; it no longer has the necessary vigor and independence. The small bourgeois simply strives to make more comfortable his petty place in the existing system of things. The animating spirit of the *petite bourgeoisie* is compromise – it compromises with Imperialism; and it compromises with Socialism; but where the compromise with Imperialism strengthens Imperialism, the compromise with Socialism weakens Socialism, softens its aggressive spirit and alters its class activity. As for the new

109

middle class, it is essentially the product of concentrated industry and Imperialism, compelled by its very nature to promote the interests of imperialistic Capitalism, directly, by openly adhering to Imperialism; indirectly, by allying itself with Socialism upon which it imposes its own reactionary purposes. The highest ideals of these two groups are bourgeois collectivism and State Capitalism. But Socialism is a revolutionary force that disrupts capitalist collectivism, that thrives by waging unrelenting war upon Capitalism and the state as unified in State Capitalism; its purposes are not expressed in a pseudo-Socialism of the state, but in the supremacy of the proletariat through industrial communism.

Socialism, accordingly, must throw off the domination and destroy the influence of these two alien groups; and it is must equally throw off the domination of skilled labor which, as a caste, becomes increasingly a part of the new middle class and of reactionary State Capitalism.

The psychology of skilled labor is the psychology of the small bourgeoisie; it thinks in terms of caste and property, and not in terms of class and solidarity of action. The property of the skilled worker is his craft and his skill, and his struggles against his employer are for the purposes of conserving this property and increasing its purchase price. [2]

The tendency of the skilled trades is to promote their interests irrespective of the rest of the workers, and often by brutal betrayal of the unorganized and the unskilled. Their unions are trusts organized to protect property; – the property vested in a skilled trade or craft. These unions, moreover, are corporate concerns, organizations of crafts which reject solidarity and co-operation with other crafts. Admission to the craft unions is limited by a variety of means, including abnormally high initiation fees. As the owner of small industrial property was concerned solely in the preservation of his property, so the skilled worker is concerned solely in the preservation of his craft skill and prestige; the concentration of industry expropriates both forms of property, but this fact, instead of creating a revolutionary psychology, intensifies the attachment to property and creates reaction in the two groups.

Originally, the slogan of skilled labor unions is, "A fair day's pay for a fair day's work." As the unions acquire political importance and the development of the industrial technology menaces the skilled crafts, a new conception arises, that of securing recognition as a part of the governing system of things. Unable to cope with the employing class industrially by means of strikes, because of industrial concentration and the decreasing value of skilled labor in the technological process the unions seek to accomplish their ends by becoming part of the government, compromising with the dominant Capitalism by means of governmental coercion. Their activity becomes more intensely that of a caste, a caste that is trying to acquire status by the hocus pocus of claiming to represent the working class. [3] The unions of skilled labor traffic in the requirement of Imperialism for a docile working class, and secure concessions by bartering away their independence and the interests of the unorganized and the unskilled. One of the reasons why State Capitalism grants a measure of recognition to the unions of the aristocracy of labor is for the purpose of using them to maintain the unskilled and the unorganized in subjection. The cleavage between the skilled and the unskilled widens.

The procedure adopted by the unions of skilled labor to secure recognition as a caste in the governing system of things is determined by circumstances; – in Germany and France by using the Socialist organizations; in the United States by bringing pressure upon the government through the political party representatives of Capitalism; in England, Australia and New Zealand by means of a labor party.

The characteristics and purposes of skilled labor find their clearest expression in Laborism. Having secured political power, Laborism becomes more than a force for securing skilled labor a place in the governing system of things; it becomes the bulwark of that system, around which rally the interests of the small bourgeoisie and the new middle class, and consequently of dominant Capitalism in its imperialistic activity. When the war broke, the Australian Labor Party was in power [4], with almost complete control of the federal and local governments. Australia immediately sent contingent after contingent of troops to "fight for liberty" in Europe; and one of the first of these contingents was used to "fight for liberty" by maintaining British rule in Egypt. With but half the population Australia provided nearly as many troops as Canada; the officials of the Labor Party gave their heartiest support and encouragement to the war and British Imperialism, proving in this respect much more zealous than the bourgeois government of Canada. The militarist, imperialist and protectionist interests of Australia are in the ascendant. Laborism directly and actively promoted the interests of Imperialism.

The policy of laborism in England has been equally reactionary. It used the war to conserve the status of the unions as a caste; it bartered away its integrity for a place in the governing system of things, and secured the place. The strikes in England during the war were generally either a revolt against the policy of Laborism or an expression of the unskilled; and where the unions of skilled labor waged strikes it was to protect its status as a caste and to maintain the unskilled and the unorganized in subjection. In its policy on war and peace the British Labor Party promoted the interests of Imperialism, justified and manufactured an ideology for the war, and became the last bulwark of defense of British Imperialism. It played fast and loose with terms of peace, and perpetrated the outrageous fraud of pretending to have declared its solidarity with revolutionary proletarian Russia, when as a matter of fact its whole program was a negation of the declarations of revolutionary Russia. In January 1918, the Labor Party opened its doors to "workers of the brain," thereby completing and emphasizing its character as a party of skilled labor, the small bourgeoisie and the new middle class, uniting to promote their interests through State Capitalism. The government of Lloyd George more and more had to depend upon British Laborism to promote the war, and the attitude of the Labor Party, as much as the attitude of the dominant Socialism and trades unions in Germany, directly discouraged and prevented revolutionary action of the great mass of the workers. There was an abandonment of the general interests of the proletariat. Labor ism in England directly and actively promoted social-Imperialism.

In this country, the American Federation of Labor pursued a policy similar to that of the trades unions in England, France and Germany. It declared for the war, and the officials of many of its affiliated unions became even more rampantly patriotic than the National Security League. It did not even flaunt the colors of the liberal bourgeoisie, but adopted an unrelenting and reactionary attitude on the war. The national bureaucracy of the AF of L acquiesced in proposals by which the workers could be cajoled from striking during the war. Gompers acted as the office boy, not of the "liberal" elements of American Capitalism, but of its most reactionary representatives. Indeed, the AF of L policy was even too reactionary for the British Labor Party and the French unions, the representatives of which vainly tried to convince Gompers and the "American Labor Mission" of the reactionary character of their attitude. Moreover, Gompers and his bureaucracy did not even show the low intelligence of British labor leaders in their dealings with the government. The British Labor Party as payment for its support of the war secured a recognized place in the government, and became a direct factor in the management of things; but the AF of L bartered away its independence and integrity and received no mess of pottage as payment. The policy of laborism results from the concept that the interests of labor depend upon the interests of capital. Where these interests clash it is assumed as being more or less accidental and incidental; their identity of interest is still the dominant factor.

As the struggles between groups in the capitalist class, often severe and bitter, do not destroy their fundamental identity of interests, so the struggle between labor and capital, according to the theory of Laborism, does not alter their identity of interest. The unions are careful that their struggles shall in no way menace Capitalism itself. The employer may be fought, but his power must not be menaced. On the field of international action, this policy is expressed in backing up the capitalist class in its projects of imperialistic expansion and wars. If our Capitalism is weakened by defeat, reasons Laborism, the unions will suffer through unemployment, longer hours and lower wages; and, therefore, Laborism promotes the interests of imperialistic Capitalism. Nationally, the policy of Laborism concerns itself simply with the interests of skilled labor and ignores the bulk of the workers, Internationally, its policy promotes the narrow interests of a nation to the exclusion of general proletarian revolutionary interests. Nationally and internationally, accordingly, Laborism betrays the cause of the proletariat. [5]

An essential characteristic of Laborism in power is that it uses the power of the state to suppress ruthlessly the strikes of the unorganized and the unskilled. But this procedure is an inevitable consequence of the psychology and status of Laborism, which is non-proletarian and has "grown into" the existing system. The industrial proletariat of unskilled labor threatens this system, and Laborism uses all its power of repression against this revolutionary class. All non-proletarian elements coalesce into one general reactionary mass against the unskilled. Laborism in action proves conclusively its non-proletarian character, and strengthens the consciousness of the unskilled, who decide upon independent action. The cleavage widens between the non-proletarian and proletarian elements among the workers, and it is the task of Socialism to intensify and organize this cleavage by arousing the independent action and emphasizing the revolutionary character of the industrial proletariat of unskilled labor – the carrier of the Social

Revolution. [6]

III

The process of concentration in industry expropriates the skill of the skilled worker by standardizing labor through the perfection of machinery. But this fact, as in the case of the small bourgeoisie, makes skilled labor even more reactionary. The unions try to maintain the prestige of their craft skill by means of their organizations, through political action, and by bringing the unskilled under their subjection. Attempts are made by the unions to organize the unskilled, but the purpose is simply to maintain the power of the crafts. The ideology of property, which is the ideology of the small bourgeoisie, continues to dominate the minds of the skilled after their "property" has been expropriated by the machine process. This ideology, in the first place, prevents the unions from generally organizing the unskilled; and, in the second place, injuriously affects those unskilled that come under the domination of the unions. Unions composed essentially of the unskilled proletariat, such as the United Mine Workers, are seduced into reaction by their affiliation with the AF of L; the bureaucracy of these unions becomes a typical craft union bureaucracy, and time and again have the mine workers been betrayed by their own officials. The unskilled ire organized, where they are organized by the AF of L, simply to protect the crafts from the ravages of the machine industry. [/] The members of craft unions have repeatedly scabbed during strikes of the unskilled in the past, when their's was the power; today, the unions make perfunctory efforts to organize for their own interests the unskilled to whom is passing the actual power in industry.

This circumstance of power is determinant. The unskilled proletariat is the typical product of modern Capitalism and controls the basic industries. This proletarian class controls equally the destiny of Capitalism and of skilled labor. The mining industry and the steel industry are dominated by the unskilled; and, except in a few cases, as for example the locomotive engineers, this is equally true of the railway industry and of transportation generally.

What are the characteristics of the proletariat of average unskilled labor? The unskilled proletariat is the industrial proletariat of standardized machine industry. An unskilled proletarian is not necessarily and always simply a worker who has no skill. The Mexican peon, the "coolie" of China, may have no skill or craft, but he is not an unskilled proletarian in the sociological sense. The unskilled proletariat is a *machine proletariat*. As Capitalism develops, the industrial process is standardized, the labor specialized. The perfection of machinery expropriates the skilled worker of his skill, as such, makes him simply a machine-minder, or drives him into minor industries where technological development lags; individual skill becomes of no importance except for a small group, and what slight aptitude may be necessary can be acquired in a few days or weeks. The worker becomes an appendage of the machine; it is no longer a skilled worker that uses the machine, but the machine uses an unskilled worker. Labor becomes average labor, standardized and specialized as an automatic factor in the machine process. The machine subjects the worker to its process; the procedure becomes mechanical, the organization systematic and standardized; standardization eliminates skill, craftsmanship, intelligence and individuality; the worker no longer has the skill of a craft: he has simply labor power, hands and muscle, and the eyes that direct these hands and muscle. A new skilled labor is created, the very small minority of engineers, superintendents, and technicians generally. The efficiency movement climaxes this development: its exponents are concerned not in the skill of the workers, but *in the regularity and standardization of their movements*. The proletariat becomes in fact a machine proletariat. [8]

The machine process dominates not a single factory or industry, but the whole of industry, integrating and standardizing the industrial system. Industry correlates itself, and if it ceases functioning at one point, the whole system feels the shock. The concentration of capital and the machine process operate jointly to unify the industrial system, in which common labor controls the working activity. Thus, while the machine process strips the worker of all skill, it simultaneously creates and places in his hands an immense power, the power of at any moment dislocating the process of production through the mass action of any considerable group of proletarians. The strikes of the unskilled unconsciously but inevitably assume the large proportions of mass revolts, including scores of thousands of workers, where the strikes of the crafts seldom did; it is easy to replace a few thousand workers at their jobs, but it is much more difficult to replace twenty or one hundred thousand. The proletariat instinctively adjusts itself to this fact.

The machine process makes a homogeneous mass out of the heterogeneous racial and religious elements; the machine process subjects the diversity of these workers to a common discipline, a common suffering, a common ideology. "By and large," says Veblen, "the technology of the machine process is a technology of action by contact." *Action by contact!* This technological fact permeates the consciousness of the unskilled workers, subtly inculcates them with the ideal of solidarity of action. The outstanding fact in the revolts of the unskilled is that they exhibit a remarkable degree of solidarity and assume revolutionary proportions and expression. The great industrial revolts of the past twenty years in this country have been revolts of the unskilled, revolts that coalesced around revolutionary organizations and activity. While the skilled were bargaining, the unskilled were fighting. Moreover, the strikes of the unskilled have been remarkably free from violence, while the craft unions have repeatedly indulged in that individual and secret violence which is characteristic of groups beaten in the social struggle. The machine process impresses upon the minds of the unskilled the value of force, of control of the industrial process, of solidarity in action; and these circumstances inevitably discourage sporadic acts of individual violence. It is the great fact and hope of the machine proletariat that, during the great strikes of the unskilled, in which men and women speaking dozens of languages participated, there was no violence on their part, no hysteria of despair, but there was determination, solidarity, the aggressive spirit of the revolution in action. The proletarian revolution is not fostered by violence, but it makes use of industrial power and organized force.

But the machine process does not simply organize the proletariat through the mechanism of production itself; it simultaneously creates a new ideology among the workers. The skilled worker thinks in terms of craft, of the individual and his property; the unskilled proletariat thinks in terms of the mass, of power, and of the *control of the machine process*. The skilled cling to craft strikes, the unskilled turn to mass action. All the facts, all the indications prove that the action of the unskilled industrial proletariat inevitably proceeds along general and revolutionary lines, that it *is* a revolutionary class. [9]

The proletariat of unskilled labor is a pariah; it has no part in the existing system, except that of a beast of burden. Its pariah position and the domination of the machine process in its ideology separate it from the rest of the community. The proletariat is out of touch with the pernicious upper class ideas that contaminate skilled labor; and the great danger is that the unions of the "aristocracy of labor" may for a time impress these ideas upon a portion of the unskilled, although the machine process itself prevents this from being permanent. All the circumstances, all the conditions, all the thoughts of this industrial proletariat place it against the existing system; its control of industry gives it the power of overthrowing that system. All other classes are arrayed against this machine proletariat, even the skilled portions of the working class. They all have contempt for this proletariat of unskilled labor; its strikes are betrayed by the skilled and crushed by the violence of the state. The unskilled proletarian has no rights except what he can conquer by his own power; he trusts no one but himself. The conditions of imperialistic Capitalism, with its merging of upper class interests into a general reactionary mass, including the aristocracy of labor, intensifies the brutality against the unskilled and the contempt in which they are held. The unskilled proletarian is determined by his very existence against the ruling system of things. Bourgeois morals, bourgeois law, bourgeois rights, are things with which he comes in contact only when they are used to oppress him,to cheat him, to drive him back to work as a slave. Is it any wonder, then, that when the unskilled proletariat acts it acts in a revolutionary way that shakes the whole social fabric? [10]

The ideology of the machine process is a vital factor in the discussion of the problems of a revolutionary class. Such a class must not only be economically in antagonism to the ruling class, it must equally develop an ideological antagonism. This ideological antagonism cannot be created simply by propaganda; it must spring out of the material conditions of the class itself. Skilled labor, after all, is a survival of the era of handicraft, and its ideology cannot be typical of the modern revolutionary class. Moreover, the attachment of the craft unionist to the property vested in his skill creates a property ideology, an ideology that psychologically affiliates skilled labor with the small bourgeoisie. Skilled labor, accordingly, cannot as yet think and act in terms of the revolution; it thinks and acts in terms of the bourgeois system of things.

It is clear, of course, that the interests of skilled labor could more advantageously be promoted by revolutionary struggle. But this requires forward vision, which skilled labor cannot develop until it emancipates itself from the psychological domination of the small bourgeoisie; and this emancipation can be achieved only by the pressure of revolutionary events from below through the action of the unskilled proletariat; only by a Socialism that, based upon the industrial proletariat of average labor, wages an uncompromising struggle against the whole Capitalist regime. Skilled labor, or what remnants of it may remain, will become a factor in the revolution only when it is compelled to align itself with and recognize the power of the great industrial proletariat. But this is not yet. Subtly, in a hundred and one ways, the craft unionist absorbs the ideology of the bourgeois order. He sees his equal, not in the common proletarian, but in the man of property. All the ideals, all the hypocrisy, all the pettiness of soul of the existing order eat away at the psychological vitals of the skilled worker. It is different with the unskilled. The material conditions and ideology of the Proletarian class unite to produce a revolutionary expression; not because it is consciously revolutionary, but because its social position drives it on toward revolutionary action as the only immediate as well as ultimate way out of its misery. The machine process is typical of modern conditions and it alone can determine a revolutionary consciousness. If the machine process affects the whole culture of our day, including science, as Veblen shows, how much more compelling must its influence be upon the minds of the men and women actually engaged in this process! The machine process creates an economic antagonism to the existing order among the proletarians; it equally creates that ideological antagonism without which a revolutionary class cannot fulfill its historic mission.

This circumstance of ideology is an important factor, the importance of which has been slighted in Socialist propaganda. [11] A revolution does not spring simply out of material conditions, but out of an ideology corresponding to these material conditions. The material conditions provide the objective forces necessary for a revolution; but this must be supplemented by the subjective force of revolutionary intensity, of an ideology that is completely alien to the ruling ideology of the nation. This ideology is not created by the revolution itself, but precedes the revolution and becomes a factor in bringing the revolution; and it is indispensable for the Socialist in theory and in practise to adapt himself to this ideology. Of course, the dominant Socialism has an ideology of its own, but it is an expression of the modes of thought of skilled labor and the small bourgeoise; no effort has been made to study and express the ideology of the basic industrial proletariat.

This new ideology finds vivid and concrete expression in the solidarity concept animating the action of the unskilled proletariat. Solidarity is a concept alien to the consciousness of the craft unionist, whose material existence creates the psychology of *laissez faire*, of being interested in his own craft interests alone. The skilled crafts usually scab upon each other; the unskilled workers, seldom. The really vital manifestations of solidarity in the American labor movement have been dominantly the expression of unskilled labor in action. In the fury produced by the betrayals of skilled labor, the unskilled occasionally scab upon the craft unions, at first; but so strong is their consciousness of solidarity that this is the exception, and not the rule. Repeatedly have the unskilled rallied to the support of the skilled during strikes; and repeatedly have they been betrayed in the settlement. An important expression of craft unionism is organized scabbery. The craft interests split the unions; the identity of occupation an conditions unites the unskilled. Instinctively, they sense in solidarity their great offensive and defensive weapon. Even the unskilled proletarians not continuously in contact with the machine process express a fine sense of solidarity, such is the compelling influence of their pariah conditions. Moreover, recent labor history shows that the only *international solidarity of labor in action has been an expression of the unskilled industrial proletariat*. The material conditions of the machine process are producing a proletariat with a sense of class solidarity without which there cannot be a Social Revolution.

As the machine process develops in scope, skilled labor comes under its influence; more and more the machine process presses the skilled down to the level of the unskilled proletariat. But this development is not sufficient to make, ideologically, a proletarian out of the skilled worker; it makes the skilled use the proletariat to artificially bolster up his declining prestige. *It is the action of the unskilled proletariat from below that will dominate the skilled workers up above.* There develops, moreover, an unskilled opposition within the unions, and the struggle becomes bitter; it is the unity of this unskilled opposition in the unions with the unorganized unskilled out of which will be forged a revolutionary labor movement, and this movement will sooner or later revolutionize the whole labor struggle. [12]

The machine proletariat of average unskilled labor constitutes the typical proletariat in the Marxian sense; it includes increasingly the overwhelming bulk of the workers, and it alone is a revolutionary class? This proletariat must constitute the material basis of Socialism. It must be awakened to consciousness and independence of action; it must be rescued from a complete or partial domination by the craft unions; it must become the driving force of Socialist propaganda and activity. On the basis of a reorganization that expresses this revolutionary class and its industrial power, Socialism alone can adopt a revolutionary attitude toward all other problems.

The class struggle, is a struggle for *power*. The class struggle itself is a form of war, social war, and *class power* decides the issue. The power of the feudal nobility lay in land; that of the bourgeoisie in money, capital; the power of the proletariat lies in its mass, in its *control of production*. This control makes the proletariat a revolutionary class, and determines the conditions of its struggle and social supremacy. Only this power can "put a bone" in Socialism, only this power can prevent Socialism losing itself in the clouds of Utopia or in the quagmires of reaction. The struggle is a struggle for power; the readjustment of Socialism is the organization and expression of the actual revolutionary class in modern society. This class is the proletarian class, the mass of unskilled labor dominating zhe industrial process of concentrated Capitalism in the new imperialistic epoch. This class emerges to consciousness, throws off equally the domination of skilled labor and the small bourgeoisie, and organizes its power for the overthrow of Capitalism. Revolutionary Socialism is the expression and synthesis of this development.

Footnotes

1. **Democracy and Organization**, by H. Laufenberg and Fritz Wolfheim.

2. A labor union is not necessarily a part of the proletarian class struggle. Not if the members aim only at immediate advantages, perhaps even at the cost of other groups of workers. – **Democracy and Organization**, by H. Laufenberg and Fritz Wolfheim.

3. The Rt. Hon. G.N. Barnes. Laborite Member of the British War Cabinet, said in an interview in November, 1917: "There are two main things which account for the [labor] unrest. One is the question of status and the other the question of wages. Of these two, the chief, to my mind, is the first."

4. The Australian Labor Government recently sent over its labor Prime Minister to England to represent its interests and as another pledge of loyalty to the Empire. The utterances of "Labor Premier" William Morris Hughes, who started his career as a particularly "revolutionary" labor leader, have met with delighted applause from the imperialistic British press, which is featuring his utterances on "organizing the Empire." Mr. Hughes was active in the Paris Trade Conference of the Allies, which met to determine ways and means of an economic war against Germany after the military war is over. He expressed himself se favoring: "A joint tax system which will establish minimum rates among the Allies and their colonies, reasonable rates for neutrals, and strong discrimination against all dealings with hostile countries." A federated empire, with a centralized War Department, aggressive militarism and Imperialism, were other British aims formulated by Mr. Hughes ... But is there any real difference between Australian Laborism and English Laborism? Superficially, yes; actually no. The apparent differences flow from the circumstance that Laborism is in power in Australia and is a negligible governmental force in England. Laborism, whether in Australia or in England, starts from the same premise : working within the bounds of the national organization, and maintaining the unity of the empire. It may be remembered that Keir Hardie refused granting independence to India. – Louis C. Fraina, "Laborism and Imperialism in Australia," in the **New Review**, June 1916. The Labor Party repudiated the excesses of its Prime Minister and other officials, but did not fundamentally alter its policy; incidentally, it may be

mentioned that even ordinary bourgeois liberals disapproved of Mr. Hughes' excesses. Prime Minister Hughes and other "Labor" officials formed a coalition with the bourgeois representatives, while the Labor Party was strongly influenced by radical currents of thought and action generated by the industrial proletariat.

5. This ideology is the ideology of Socialism wherever its councils are dominated by skilled labor. Wolfgang Heine represented this "Socialist Laborism" when in a speech on February 22, 1915, he said: "Our working people live from industry. Especially from export trade. If this is destroyed, the worker will be more damaged than the employer. The capitalist can take his money away and put it in other undertakings, even abroad. The worker, if he has no more work, is ruined. It has been said, 'What difference does it make whether the worker has any longer a living in Germany? He emigrates and expends his labor power elsewhere.' That is no longer such a simple affair, and our German working people are too good to serve as fertilizer for foreign civilization. In spite of all conflicts with the present state, the worker it bound to it."

6. In New Zealand, the Labor Party repeatedly betrayed the unskilled, and these betrayals finally resulted in the formation of a new proletarian party, the Social Democratic Party. Five years ago the United Federation of Labor, which practically adopted the IWW preamble, prepared for a general strike, relying chiefly upon seamen, dock laborers and miners. The strike was betrayed by skilled labor, which deserted. Moreover, the United Labor Party issued a manifesto against the strike, and this betrayal was one of the chief causes of the strike's failure. Skilled labor, its unions and its party, joined hands with the employers and strikebreakers.

7. Briefly, the organization of the unskilled is not compatible with the AF of L, for the reason that the latter in its essentials is a federation of individual crafts, whereas the unskilled cannot by any means be so classed ... The consciousness that they [the unskilled] cannot achieve their solidarity with the American Federation of Labor is one of the chief reasons why they do not join the United Laborers' Locals which have been instituted in their special behalf. They know that there is no identity of interest between themselves and the craft organizations; that the latter will use them when it is convenient to do so, otherwise they will repudiate them or will refuse to make any effort to help them gain better conditions. – Austin Lewis, *Organization of the*

Unskilled, in the **New Review**, November, 1913.

8. The share of the operative workman in the machine industry is typically that of an attendant, an assistant, whose duty it is to keep pace with the machine process and to help out with workmanlike manipulation at points where the machine process engaged is incomplete. His work supplements the machine process, rather than makes use of it. On the contrary, the machine process makes use of the workman. The ideal mechanical contrivance is the automatic machine. Perfection in the machine technology is attained in the degree in which the given process can dispense with manual labor; whereas perfection in the handicraft system means perfection of manual workmanship. It is the part of the workman to know the working of the mechanism in which he is associated and to adapt his movements with mechanical accuracy to its requirements. – Thorstein Veblen, **The Instinct of Workmanship**.

9. This great fact was proven and emphasized during the proletarian revolution in Russia. The moderate socialists, the Mensheviki, representing the dominant Socialism, largely expressed skilled labor and the small Bourgeoisie; while the great strength of the Bolsheviki lay in their influence among the industrial workers, the unskilled proletariat. The railway unions, dominated officially by the skilled workers, acted in favor of the revolution to overthrow Czarism, but they acted against the proletarian revolution as expressed in the Bolshevist movement; and when the revolutionary proletarian government dissolved the Constituent Assembly, because it was counter-revolutionary, representative of the bourgeois democracy of all the classes and an expression of the parliamentary system that the revolution must necessarily annihilate, the railway unions opposed the Bolsheviki and supported the Constituent Assembly. The Social. Revolution can be carried through only by the industrial proletariat of unskilled labor, in spite of and acting against all the ideas and activity of all other social groups. The circumstance that individuals, even if in considerable numbers, may migrate from one class to another, does not alter the character or interests of the classes.

10. The machine process tends to widen the gulf between the possessing and the revolutionary classes ... The proletariat, or at least that nucleus of it Which we have pointed out as being engaged in the machine process, actually does tend to become more and more revolutionary, that is, to take up a continually more iconoclastic

attitude to the natural rights theories. – Austin Lewis, **The Militant Proletariat**.

11. The vital thing to us as men of action, as seers of a new vision of life, is to analyze and interpret the psychological reaction of the workers to their conditions of existence; the emotional temper produced by machine industry, the new type of mind, of men, of outlook upon life being developed ... The literature of Socialism abounds with phrases concerning "proletarian psychology," and ''proletarian modes of thought." But these terms are simply convenient phrases with no concrete meaning. This literature deals thoroughly and magnificently with the material conditions determining the consciousness of men; but scarcely an effort is being made to analyze that consciousness itself, particularly the changes wrought therein by the changing social existence. The philosophical system of Marx recognizes the immense power of psychological factors in history. Maix stressed the importance of human effort and the human factor. In his **Poverty of Philosophy** Marx scored Proudhon for not understanding that "social relations are as much produced by men as are the cloth, linen, etc. ... The same men who establish social relations in conformity with their material productivity, produce also the principles, the ideals, the categories conformably with their social relations." In the **Eighteenth Brumaire of Louis Bonaparte**: "Man makes his own history." In one of his fragmentary notes on Feuerbach, Marx indicates the dynamic role of the individual in the revolution: "The materialistic doctrine that men are the products of conditions and education, different men, therefore, the products of other conditions and changed education, forgets that circumstances may be altered by men, and that the educator has himself to be educated." The importance Marx attached to the human factor emphasizes itself in **Capital**: "By thus acting on the external world and changing it he [man] at the same time changes his own nature. He develops his slumbering powers, and compels them to act in obedience to his own sway." *Man changes his own nature.* Are not these changes as important as, perhaps more important than, the social conditions producing these changes? ... The value of psychology is greater than the simple analysis of social problems. As social conditions are transformed, men are transformed; and the supreme utility of psychology lies in the analysis of the transformation in the nature of man ... Economics has given us a vision of the new society; psychology will give us a vision of the new

126

humanity. – Louis C. Fraina, *Socialism and Psychology*, in **The New Review**, May 1, 1915.

12. During this struggle, the question of industrial union organization crops up in the unions, and ends in a miserable compromise in the form of "amalgamation." Moreover, the "industrial" form is adopted only if the skilled crafts can maintain the unskilled in subjection. At the 1914 Congress of German Labor Unions, the executive committee reported: "Labor Union development is undeniably in the direction of the amalgamation of organizations into great and powerful unions, and technical evolution more than ever requires the entrance of helpers and unskilled into the trade and industrial unions to which they are eligible." The Factory Workers' Union, composed of unskilled machine workers, proposed the following amendment: "And also the entrance of skilled workers in the unions of the unskilled for which they are eligible." The amendment was defeated, and the executive committee's recommendation of an arbitration court was adopted. The factory workers thereupon made a statement re-affirming their claim to the skilled workers in establishments under their control and called the proposed court a "compulsory arbitration court." The transport workers and unskilled workers generally manifested a decidedly oppositional tendency. In the existing unions the unskilled are a minority, and it is only by contact with the unorganized unskilled that they can dominate the industrial situation.

Chapter IX
Class and Nation

REVOLUTIONARY Socialism adopts a policy of unrelenting antagonism toward nationalism in fully-developed capitalist nations, (only in pre-capitalistic nations that are the objectives of Imperialism, such as Egypt, China and India, is nationalism progressive). This is an acceptance of the fact that our attitude towards the nation is a decisive factor in the readjustment of Socialism; and our attitude towards the nation carries with it the reconstruction of our national and international policy, not simply in relation to war, but to the whole scope of the movement.

The nation is an historical product, and its significance and our attitude are determined by the prevailing historical conditions. It is this circumstance that makes necessary our opposition to nationalism in highly-developed imperialistic countries, and our favoring nationalism in the revolutionary sense in the pre-capitalistic countries that are the objectives of Imperialism.

The nation did not come into being because of mystical or cultural impulses; it was the product of a definite process of economic and class development, and its political reflex. Being the product of an historical process, it is futile to discuss whether the nation is or is not desirable in itself; the necessity of the nation, its character and function, are determined by the prevailing stage of social development. The nation, as such, is neither democratic nor reactionary in tendency, this depends upon the historical *milieu* and the social forces it expresses; under certain conditions the nation is progressive, under other conditions it may be compellingly reactionary. An important point to be stressed in our attitude toward the nation, accordingly, is the fundamental difference between the democratic nationalism of the era of bourgeois revolution and the reactionary nationalism of imperialistic Capitalism. Eduard

Bernstein has proposed that Socialists oppose the "new capitalistic nationalism which culminates in Imperialism," and not the "old ideology" of nationalism "which required the self-government of the nation as a centre of culture among other similar centres." [1] Bernstein's proposal neglects the economic and political aspects of the problem as determined by the development of Imperialism and its reactionary character. His attitude is abstract, and not realistic. Bernstein admits that nationalism culminates in Imperialism, but a certain cultural beauty in nationalism is dear to his soul: the proletarian revolution, however, sets its face toward the future, not the past. Imperialism annihilates "self-government of the nation" and its cultural value, and the struggle becomes a struggle for Socialism, which solves all problems. Moreover, it is no longer possible, it is even undesirable from the standpoint of the proletarian revolution, to revive the democratic ideology of nationalism, since the social conditions underlying its previous existence are not now dominant in the economy of industrially highly developed nations, and since it is an ideology not at all compatible with the emancipation of the proletariat. The emphasis laid upon democratic nationalism leaves unconsidered the fact that Capitalism has turned its back upon the era of democratic aspirations, and that consequently the contemporary expression of nationalism is undemocratic and reactionary. And if we favor nationalism in pre-capitalistic countries, it is because nationalism there is a revolutionary factor and an historical necessity in the struggle against Imperialism: the necessity of national wars of liberation is recognized by Socialism, and colonial uprisings are national wars in the making. Whatever cultural value may inhere in the nation will be retained and released for further development by the proletarian revolution, which establishes a society internationally united, but which, being communistic, decrees the utmost in national, racial and local autonomy, initiative and individuality.

What is the nation, and what are its characteristic forms

in the development of society?

The nation, the trend toward the nation, makes its appearance with Capitalism. Ascending Capitalism develops the nation-state, which plays an important part in the overthrow of Feudalism, is, in fact, one of its consequences. The effort to break the fetters placed upon industry organized on the basis of the city-state leads directly to the formation of the nation state. Ascending Capitalism requires freedom of trade within as large a territorial unit as possible, national markets exclusively for the national bourgeoisie to develop and exploit; a common system of coinage, weights and measures; and a strong central government to maintain order, foster industry, and carve out the territorial limits of the nation. The nation-state develops a sense of solidarity in the people of a particular national group, and firmly establishes national institutions, a national literature and culture, and a national bourgeoisie. The nation conforms essentially to economic and geographical facts ; while race and language have been convenient expressions of the nation, the nation has itself created "race" and "language," and often suppressed or amalgamated them in the fulfillment of its historic mission.

The early struggles of ascending Capitalism seek to create the national unit along as large territorial limits as possible, while maintaining order within the national domain. The industrialized unit within the developing nation seeks wider markets, new sources of raw materials, regions which it can bring within the sway of the internal market. The earlier process of expansion is accelerated by a series of bloody wars. All this, in conjunction with other favoring circumstances, including the growing power of the bourgeoisie and the decay of the feudal nobility, leads to the institution of absolute monarchy, directly traceable to the requirements of the bourgeoisie. The bourgeoisie at this period, and after, is revolutionary, its revolutionary expressions assuming vitality in the measure that the carving out of the national frontiers is completed. But, this task accomplished, the social and political organization

131

expressed in the dominance of absolute monarchy, itself based upon a compromise between bourgeoisie and feudal nobility, becomes a very real obstacle to the development of the forces of production. In the effort to destroy this obstacle, the bourgeoisie initiates a more intensive revolutionary era, one result of which is the organization of the nation along democratic and republican, or semi republican lines. It is at this epoch that the nation assumes a definite and mature expression.

But the bourgeoisie becomes frightened of its own revolutionary impulses: bourgeois revolutions end in dictatorships, – which persist or disintegrate as conditions determine. Having accomplished the task of destroying the economic fetters upon its development, the bourgeoisie becomes largely indifferent to the *form* of government, as long as scope is allowed its economic development; questions of the form of government become means of expression for rival bourgeois group interests, issues in the immature struggles of the workers, and in older nations means of intrigue for the remnants of the feudal nobility. Fear of the proletariat, competition between nations, struggles of various groups within the ruling class itself, – all these and other circumstances incline the bourgeoisie toward "strong" government, leaving a merely sentimental and theoretical feeling for general liberal principles. A compromise is struck in constitutional monarchy or an oligarchical republic. In this process of developing the nation, bourgeois revolutions and liberal ideas are an incidence. When the bourgeoisie has completed the industrial revolution and established its supremacy, it discards liberal ideas and retains only that irreducible minimum necessary for social control. The minimum varies as historical requirements vary; but bourgeois democracy persists, until the era of Imperialism establishes a new autocracy, comparable in its fundamentals, if not in its forms, to the absolute monarchy.

In nations which completed their national bourgeois revolution sufficiently prior to the era of modern Imperialism to allow their democratic ideas scope for ascendancy, the reaction

132

against liberal ideas was only partially successful. But in nations which completed their national revolution almost simultaneously with the advent of Imperialism, or which emerged into the modern era of Capitalism without such a revolution, democracy in government never established itself. Germany is the classic type of this development, with Japan a remarkably close parallel. The bourgeois revolution in Germany in 1848 was crushed by the cowardly hesitancy and treason of the middle class, the revolution being uncompromisingly adhered to only by the developing proletariat. National unity was achieved not as a revolt against the feudal class, but in a compromise with the feudal class of junkers. Bourgeois democracy did not materialize, and was lost. The industrial revolution strengthened, instead of weakening, the monarchical power. But the reaction against democracy might have proven temporary, as in previous periods, (the forces of "democracy" grew steadily, a whole movement, the Social Democracy, being devoted almost solely to the task of completing the bourgeois revolution,) had not a new set of circumstances intervened which, instead of finding an expression in the overthrow of autocracy, found its interests in the perpetuation of autocracy, – the advent of Imperialism. Germany was united in 1871, and a decade later its imperialistic era began; and this let loose all those reactionary tendencies which lead to a capitalist revival of autocracy in one form or another. Where "democratic" nations had to create a new autocracy, Germany simply adapted its prevailing autocracy to the new conditions.

Imperialism assumes objectively the form of a struggle for the control of territory rich in natural resources and capable of being industrially revolutionized by an industrial nation undertaking the work of "development." Capitalism in the imperialistic era turns in on itself and in a certain way reproduces the period of its youth, when it struggled for a similar territorial objective, – with this difference, however: that where the former struggle created the nation, the contemporary struggle *negates* the nation. [2] This process carries with it an accessory fact: as the earlier struggles of Capitalism produced war and absolute monarchy, so today Imperialism not only produces war, but a tendency toward "strong" government, – autocracy disguised under a variety of political forms.

There is an assumption among some Socialists that, while the nation is the particular creation and form of expression of the bourgeoisie, the nation is just as necessary as the class, that it is a separate factor, and that the struggles of nation against nation as such function as dynamically as class struggles. History refutes the assumption: *national struggles are a form of expression of the class struggle*.

The historical generalizations concerning this problem may be summarized as follows:

1. The nation is the expression of a particular social and economic system and the class representing that system, – historically, the era of competitive Capitalism and the bourgeoisie.
2. The course of a nation is determined by the development of the economics of its social system and ruling class.
3. Competing nations represent competing social economic systems and ruling class interests.
4. The hegemony of a nation at any particular epoch represents the hegemony of the most highly developed social system, consequently most powerful ruling class.
5. The struggle between nations – national struggles – are an expression of a struggle between rival ruling classes using the nation in waging their disputes.
6. In the era of Imperialism, these struggles between nations become active aspects of the class struggle against the proletariat, as "national" imperialistic wars have a general tendency to increase and intensify the exploitation of the proletariat and break up the proletarian movement by strengthening the class position of the capitalist. The ultimate objective of Imperialism is world power, and this power is to exploit

more intensively the proletariat. While, accordingly, Imperialism and imperialistic wars are struggles of bourgeoisie against bourgeoisie, they are simultaneously and more fundamentally a single struggle against the proletariat.

These are the generalizations; the practice is not as concrete. Social progress is uneven ; nations do not develop simultaneously, although their development is along essentially parallel lines; remnants of the preceding social system persist into the new and affect events; a ruling class often disputes supremacy with, its predecessor or potential successor, and is itself often divided into warring groups; nor is Capitalism static, its various stages of development being a distinct factor and affecting the course of events. Then, again, the nation, a product of historic factors, becomes itself an historic factor, and at times must be considered as a distinct category. But all the historic factors are synthesized in the dominance of class and the struggle of class against class, and are fundamentally determined by the process of the class struggle.

The series of bloody wars which signalized the advent of the bourgeoisie and the nation-state was essentially the expression of the class interests of the bourgeoisie in conflict with Feudalism. The struggles of many years between France and England, marked by the battles of Crecy, Poitiers and Agincourt, were fundamentally a class struggle in the form of war between the rising bourgeoisie of England struggling for territorial conquest and markets, and the Feudalism of France, – the triumph of the English yeomanry over the flower of the French nobility is symbolical of the character of the wars. It is true that England and France at this period had much in common, historically, both being at the era of territorial consolidation, politically a distinguishing feature of the formation of the nation. But England was much more advanced than France economically, its bourgeoisie having acquired a larger share of power, the commercial interests stronger; while in France Feudalism was still largely unshaken by the bourgeoisie. The flourishing manufacturing interests of England were encouraged and protected by the government, and the extensive trade in wool with the manufacturing towns of Flanders was a direct cause of the wars. Undoubtedly, these wars were not purely capitalist wars, feudal interests being involved; but what distinguishes them from previous wars and gives them their distinctive historic character was the emergence of bourgeois interests. The national struggles of the era of the Reformation were another expression of the interests of the class struggle of the bourgeoisie. The Reformation was a revolt against the "universal empire" of Rome and a factor in the development of the nation, a product of the national impulses of the oncoming bourgeois social system ; the wars it let loose were national wars waged to destroy the moral, political and economic system of Feudalism as synthesized in the Papacy: they were wars that promoted bourgeois class interests in the process of securing social supremacy.

The wars of the French Revolution offer the finest illustration of the essentially class character of the nation and its wars. These wars were an extension and continuation of the struggle waged by the bourgeoisie within France against the absolute monarchy and Feudalism. The revolution that overthrew the monarchy and its remaining feudal relations struck a terrific blow at monarchy and Feudalism throughout Europe. Clearly and absolutely, the national struggles that followed were determined by class interests – the class interests of the bourgeoisie, incarnated in France, in conflict with the class interests of Feudalism, incarnated in monarchical Europe. The class struggle waged by the bourgeoisie in France by means of revolution was converted into an *international* class struggle waged by means of war. The revolutionary and Napoleonic wars were the death-grapple of two social-economic systems struggling for supremacy. [3]

The class struggle is a struggle between a dominant economic system and its ruling class, and a rising economic system and its class representative. The national struggles cited were of this character, – struggles between Feudalism and Capitalism, each seeking control, a struggle, moreover, which was proceeding equally within the states representing feudal interests. But once all states become bourgeois nations, the national struggles become struggles of the same ruling class for international supremacy, – national bourgeoisie against national bourgeoisie, as in the great clash between Napoleonic France and England. This struggle between bourgeois nations waged in the form of war is as much an aspect of the class struggle as the struggles between groups of the ruling class within a nation. This is particularly so in the struggles of Imperialism.

An important phase of Capitalism is the expropriation of the capitalist by the capitalist. In national economics this expropriation proceeds by means of concentration of industry and centralization of capital. But Capitalism reaches a point where, along with other factors, this process of expropriation develops into a higher form. Expropriation and concentration along national lines become insufficient; big capital and small capital compromise through monopoly and State Capitalism; and instead of the expropriation of the individual capitalist within the nation there comes the struggle to expropriate the capitalist class of another nation by means of diplomatic pressure, Imperialism and war. The process of expropriation assumes a new aspect: it becomes dominantly international, instead of national.

The national struggles of Imperialism, accordingly, are struggles of class against class, of bourgeoisie against bourgeoisie for the robbery and mastery of the world.

But these struggles are equally and more dynamically aspects of the proletarian class struggle, imposing the necessity of an uncompromising war of the proletariat against Imperialism and the imperialistic nation. The struggle of nation against nation converts itself into a struggle of proletariat against bourgeoisie, in which the relative class power decides the issue. A victorious imperialistic nation strengthens its class power not only against a rival bourgeoisie, *but as against its own proletariat and the proletariat in the countries it has acquired for "development."* The "penetration" of capital in new territory subjects new peoples, a new proletariat, to the rule of capital, to the system of capitalist exploitation; and the significance of this new system is not simply in added numbers of exploitable workers, but in an increase of power of the capitalist, an altering of the relations of class power in the older capitalist countries to the disadvantage of the proletariat. It is quite obvious that a general imperialistic war oppresses the proletariat; but this general war was prepared by a series of minor, colonial wars, by years of imperialistic exploitation, during a period when the workers of capitalistic nations tolerated the subjection of colonial peoples because of a smug and illusory sense of accruing "prosperity." The general capitalist tendency is to impose the rule of capital over the whole world; the ultimate stake of Imperialism is world power, and this power depends upon the subjection and exploitation of the proletariat, furthering and intensifying this subjection and exploitation. A general imperialistic war is fundamentally, accordingly, a phase of the class struggle waged by the capitalist class against the workers of the world.

In two senses, then, are national struggles today class struggles: they are, incidentally, struggles of bourgeois class against bourgeois class for world supremacy; and they are, fundamentally, struggles for the subjection of the proletariat.

As an expression of the bourgeoisie, the nation must conform to the requirements of bourgeois supremacy. Imperialism is a revolt against the national fetters placed upon the development of the productive forces. Capitalism has developed a world economy, the parts of which are dependent each upon the other. The world is agonizing in the contradiction of a world economy which national states are trying to bend to their purposes to promote the profits of the national bourgeoisie. The only method conceivable to Capitalism is Imperialism, – the extension of the limits of the nation by fire and sword and the annexation of as much new territory as possible within a particular nation. But when this is done, the nation ceases as a nation, and a political monstrosity takes its place. The great, the overwhelming fact is that the nation has out-lived its usefulness, that it is now decrepit as an economic and political entity. The bourgeoisie itself is in revolt against the nation, its own particular product: and against international Imperialism the proletariat must oppose international Socialism.

Imperialism fundamentally excludes the democratic federation of nations. The increasing volume of surplus-values develops the capitalist necessity of rivalry and destruction. Imperialistic Capitalism is compelled to discover new means of waste, of destruction, it must throw the world into continual and increasingly gigantic struggles to perpetuate itself. Capitalism has generated the forces of internationality; it remains for Socialism, however, to effectively organize the forces into a world-state through proletarian communism. It is inconceivable that Capitalism should produce an actual unity of nations, which would have to include those nations and territory that are objectives of Imperialism, and pre-suppose the dissolution of the nation in its present bourgeois form and the abandonment of national-imperialistic interests, – and that, clearly, means the end of capitalist domination. Identically as with parliamentary government, the nation is the particular form of expression of Capitalism. Capitalism finds its essential expression in the nation and parliamentary government; the proletariat in the world-state and industrial government.

The nation, or nationality, will remain as a cultural, ideological and psychological fact; its economic and political necessity has passed away. And it is this cultural and psychological fact that confuses the problem of the nation in the eyes of many. The Socialist does not deny that the nation has performed a cultural mission, but as a phase of the general process of human development. Whatever of cultural value may inhere in the nation, or nationality, will persist under Socialism, just as the proletarian revolution, in annihilating Capitalism, does not annihilate that which is of value in Capitalism. Socialism is the cultural heir of the ages. At the present moment, however, the greatest menace to these cultural contributions lies in the perpetuation of the nation in its bourgeois, imperialistic form, symbol of a decrepit industrial and social system.

In the coming decisive struggles against Capitalism, revolutionary Socialism recognizes and emphasizes that the class struggle determines all our action – that the national ideology is a fetter upon the emancipation of the proletariat – and that the Social Revolution is international in scope and purpose.

Footnotes

1. Eduard Bernstein. *Revisionism and Nationalism*, in the New Review, Sepember 1, 1915.

2. The negation of the nation is not peculiar to German Imperialism: it is an attribute of all Imperialism. An Italian imperialist declaims as follows: "It remains for us to conquer. It is said that all the other territories are 'occupied.' But there have never been any territories *res nullius*. Strong nations, or nations on the path of progress, conquer nations in decadence." British domination in Egypt was established at a period when Egypt was on the verge of a national revival, and the British have ruthlessly suppressed national aspirations and unity, as they have in India. Turkey has the necessary materials for becoming a strong modern nation; but the Great Powers have consciously and brutally kept it in a state of decadence, – all because of imperialistic interests. This is the identical policy being pursued in China.

3. The supremacy of Napoleon and the national uprisings that finally accomplished his overthrow, do not alter this interpretation. Under Napoleon the struggle gradually assumed a new form: the class interests and national interests of the European bourgeoisie, which the Napoleonic wars had stirred into life by riding rough-shod over feudal institutions, fought against the plans of France to establish an hegemony in Europe and subordinate other nations to its interests. The very factor that underlay the Napoleonic epoch, the destruction of

feudal relations wherever the French armies conquered, at the same time developed the force that overthrew Napoleon – the more definite emergence of the nation and its bourgeois character. At this stage, the struggle was essentially between rival groups of the same ruling class in different nations: the struggle between England and Napoleon was of this character, England participating in the wars against Napoleon not to conserve monarchy in Europe, but to protect its industrial and commercial supremacy.

Chapter X
Problems of State Capitalism

IMPERIALISTIC State Capitalism emphasizes the fact of the state, of government, being an economic agency of the ruling class. State and capitalist industry, government and ruling class, become one and indivisible. This was not completely the case in the era of competitive Capitalism. The influence of persisting feudal remnants and bourgeois class immaturity, compelled the state to adopt a policy, so to say, of maintaining the "balance of power" between rival groups of the ruling class itself, a state of things determining the earlier manifestations of the workers' struggles; and precisely because of these divisions the state was occasionally in the position of asserting its supremacy as against the diversity of ruling class interests. Today, the conditions of Imperialism have created a *bloc* of ruling class interests, an amalgam of Capitalism that functions through the state and which makes the state completely and consciously the agency of dominant Capitalism and the groups it has forced into its service. State Capitalism, accordingly, is not an abandonment of Capitalism: it is a strengthening of Capitalism – Capitalism at the climax of its development.

The larger part of Socialist propaganda and practice in the past have been making for State Capitalism, often euphoniously and misleadingly designated as State Socialism. Whenever the state nationalized an industry, whenever the state imposed its control over industry, the Socialist majority naively accepted this as an abandonment of Capitalism, as a symptom of the growing importance of Socialism and the transformation of Capitalism into Socialism. Simple souls! What was passing was not Capitalism, but the competitive *laissez faire* era of Capitalism; what came was not Socialism nor an "installment" of Socialism, but imperialistic State Capitalism, the most brutal and typical expression of capitalist power and supremacy. Socialist propaganda, including largely Socialist thought, did not adapt itself to the development of Capitalism, did not adapt itself to the new conditions and requirements arising out of this development. Socialism is not state ownership or management of industry, but the opposite: Socialism annihilates the state. Not even should Socialism conquer the state and maintain itself, proceeding to nationalize industry, would that be Socialism: when Socialism conquers, its first act is to abolish the state, its parliamentary regime and forms of activity. Socialism, it must be emphasized, annihilates the state; industry is not transformed into the state, but state and industry, as now constituted, are transformed into proletarian communism, functioning industrially and socially through new administrative norms of the organized producers, and not through the state. [1]

Revolutionary Socialism rejects the bourgeois policy of state ownership, rejects State Capitalism as a phase of Socialism, and insists upon *proletarian management* through industrial communism.

The conditions of State Capitalism emphasize this revolutionary policy; the antagonism between state and Socialism is intensified, compelling the separation of Socialism from an industrial policy of the imperialistic state, and in this sense directly promotes the revolution.

State Capitalism is not Socialism and never can become Socialism. It may promote the coming of Socialism, but only indirectly through intensifying the antagonism of the proletariat toward the bourgeois state, and by compelling Socialism to adopt a policy of industrial communism. The "nationalization" of industry is a Socialist measure, a measure making for Socialism, only when introduced as a temporary measure of the dictatorship of the proletariat, the first act of which is to lay a dictatorial hand upon the forces of production in the process of crushing the old regime and introducing the communist system of Socialism. State Capitalism makes for Socialism in this sense, as with Imperialism, that it climaxes the development of Capitalism and broadens and deepens class antagonisms; but as

Imperialism must necessarily be struggled against for its overthrow, so State Capitalism is a factor in the coming of Socialism by arousing a new and more intense struggle against the whole of bourgeois society. The institutional developments of Capitalism do not bring, they never can bring, Socialism; they function in the process simply as they develop the proletarian struggle against these institutions and all institutions of capitalist society. State Capitalism is not Socialism and never can become Socialism precisely because it is a state proposition; Socialism is determined in a struggle to annihilate the state as a necessary instrument of revolution and as a means of developing the new communist society which negates the "state" in the bourgeois sense.

State Capitalism accentuates and sharpens class divisions, by arraying against the industrial proletariat all other class groups merged and expressed in the new state. As against the general reactionary mass of ruling class interests, the proletariat stands as a class thrown by the very conditions of its existence against the unified capitalist regime. State Capitalism regulates and directs capital and labor; it seeks to realize the Utopia of peace between the classes, of the abolition, or at least suspension, of the class struggle. [2] This regulation may, in a measure, prove onerous to the capitalist, but is accepted as the necessary condition for the progressive promotion of his interests; it proves in large measure onerous to the proletariat, and as it cannot be merged in State Capitalism the proletariat is driven to revolt against the state and Capitalism as unified in the new scheme of things.

The policy of revolutionary Socialism is neither to oppose nor to advocate the coming of State Capitalism. Either policy would be futile, and reactionary. State Capitalism is a fact and Socialism must adjust itself to the fact. Socialism organizes the aggressive struggle against State Capitalism as the synthetic expression of the whole capitalist regime. The problem of revolutionary Socialism is to develop the consciousness and class power of the proletariat, to throw the proletariat against Capitalism in struggle after struggle determined by the immediate and ultimate requirements of revolutionary action. The antagonism between State Capitalism and Socialism is emphasized by sharply distinguishing between the two and by the action of the proletariat itself. The policy of State Capitalism of regulating labor, and in this way to prevent if not actually prohibit strikes, rouses the action of the workers; a strike under these conditions becomes a strike directed against the state; a strike, accordingly, becomes a class act of political importance. More and more it becomes clear that strikes are not simply directed against the employer or against the state, but against the unified capitalist regime as organized in State Capitalism, and that it is this regime against which the struggle must be consciously directed. The process of state regulation is met by the Socialist process of arousing in the proletariat the consciousness of its control of industry. The proletariat sets itself against the state, the state against the proletariat; the struggle becomes more intense and general, the antagonisms more acute and irreconcilable. As the state imposes its control over industry, the proletariat challenges that control, contests the authority and force of the state, and itself gradually acquires the power of control over industry. The challenge under the impulse of events develops into the Social Revolution.

The Social Revolution becomes a fact when the proletariat has acquired sufficient consciousness of its control over industry to establish that control in practice. The proletariat, accordingly, develops a state within the state, develops the norms of the future Socialist society within the structure of Capitalism. The central factor in this is the industrial organization of the proletariat, partly actual through industrial unions, partly ideological through the conception of the necessity of overthrowing the state and substituting for it a society of communistically organized producers, – the proletariat functioning in industry and becoming aware of its strategic power. [3] It is this proletarian control, organized and unorganized, that constitutes equally the force for the overthrow of State Capitalism and its social system, and the basis of the Socialist society of the future.

A lure that will be offered the workers is the struggle to "democratize" State Capitalism through Socialist parliamentary activity. This constitutes in a new form the old conception of "growing into" Socialism, – transforming State Capitalism into Socialism by "democratizing" the government, placing it in the hands of "the people." This policy is equally condemnable as strategy and tactics, – as strategy, it dispenses with the necessity of overthrowing the state as an indispensable phase of the Social Revolution; as tactics, it strengthens the state and weakens the proletariat by obscuring the fact that its power resides in control of the industrial process. Moreover, State Capitalism is fundamentally and necessarily undemocratic; it cannot be democratized, it must be abolished by the proletarian revolution. The coming of Socialism is a process of violent and implacable struggles, not a dress parade of amicable transformation. The concept of "transformation" in practise doesn't transform Capitalism, it transforms the proletarian movement into a caricature of Socialism and a prop of Capitalism. The proletariat is concerned, not indirectly with the forms of administration of State Capitalism, but directly in developing its forces for the immediate struggle against and the ultimate overthrow of State Capitalism. Socialism is not a struggle for democracy; it is a struggle for proletarian power The only democracy compatible with the requirements of the proletariat is the democracy of communist Socialism, a democracy arising out of the total destruction of bourgeois democracy. The only immediate democracy that concerns the proletariat is the democracy of its dynamic struggles, the democracy of its own industrial unions and mass action.

Revolutionary Socialism rejects "co-operation" with the capitalist, in industry as in politics. One phase of State Capitalism is the policy of trying to maintain industrial peace, and this is attempted alternately by coercion and cajolery. One means of cajolery is an arrangement by which the workers may "co-operate" with the employers in the consideration of matters affecting a particular industry or factory. [4] The state tries to compel this co-operation, making it an impliedly compulsory affair, and it becomes the function of the government to bring the workers under the sway of the capitalist in ways that strike at the independent action of the proletariat. Autocracy in government is supplemented by a sham democracy in industry, by apparently giving the workers a share in the regulation of their conditions, but which actually is an illusion, as the power of the employers sets it at naught. The purpose is to run the militant spirit of the workers into the ground, to disorganize their independent action.

A development of this character is the proposal, recently adopted by the British government, for the formation of National Industrial Councils, to be established in each industry by the government and which are to consist of employers and employees, acting under the control of the state. This is an attempt at general and definite "class co-operation" which would inevitably react against the proletariat. Moreover, it is in a measure prompted by the hope that through this means British capital may cajole labor to accept lower wages after the war on the plea that it is necessary to meet the new competition. These councils would be dominated by the capitalist interests, as against the workers would be arrayed state and employers and their joint power; they would strengthen the reactionary influence of the bureaucracy within the craft unions, and as a matter of fact many British union officials are enthusiastic about the proposal, while there is considerable opposition developing among the workers and the more radical unions. Finally, such industrial councils would obviously and dominantly be used by the skilled minority against the unskilled workers, and this is undoubtedly one of the driving purposes behind the proposal. In its attitude toward the workers, State Capitalism adopts and emphasizes the policy of "divide and conquer." All proposals for a sham industrial democracy are useless and dangerous; they are schemes directed at the independence and action of the proletariat, aiming to subordinate the proletarian to the capitalist. They foster the illusion of a measure of industrial democracy under Capitalism granted by grace of the capitalist: the only measure of industrial democracy that the proletariat can secure under Capitalism must be conquered by itself, maintained and extended through its industrial unions, strikes and general mass action, which impose its will upon employer and government.

The revolutionary proletariat, accordingly, rejects equally the lure of "democratizing" the government of State Capitalism and the lure of a "share" in the regulation of labor conditions through the fraudulent pretense of "industrial democracy."

The proletariat uses all its action, industrial and parliamentary, to develop its class power and strike at State Capitalism, and to secure an immediately partial and ultimately complete control of industry.

State Capitalism emphasizes the fact that Capitalism is not transformed into Socialism by the development of bourgeois institutions, but by the development of proletarian consciousness and class power out of which arise the norms of the institutions of the oncoming communist society.

It is only because the meaning of political action has been misunderstood or disguised by petty bourgeois Socialism that its function is conceived as being the "democratizing" of State Capitalism into Socialism. Political action, in the Marxian sense, is the general revolutionary action of the proletariat. An industrial revolt, a mass strike, are as much a political act as participation in the parliamentary activity of the state. There is no more complete proof of the petty bourgeois character of the dominant Socialism than its narrow interpretation and practice of political action. [5] In the actual practice of the Socialist movement, political action has become a dead and deadening parliamentarism, – the "parliamentary idiocy" bitterly satirized by Marx, "that fetters those whom it infects to an imaginary world, and robs them of all sense, all remembrance, all understanding of the rude outside world." Parliamentarism is simply one phase of political action; political action is a process which, in the revolutionary sense and as a factor in the overthrow of Capitalism, is and includes all forms of militant class action of the proletariat. Socialist political action is a process of revolution; it is in this sense that "all class struggles are political struggles," political in the sense that the class struggle is directed against the existing social system and its governmental expression. The conquest of political power is not the parliamentary penetration of the state, but the developing class power of the proletariat that yields it social supremacy. Parliamentarism is a phase, and not at all a dominant phase, of revolutionary political action; it is utterly reactionary when it separates itself, as it has done, from the general action of the proletariat, when it seeks to dominate, instead of being dominated by, the general struggles of the workers. Under the conditions of State Capitalism, parliamentarism alone and of itself becomes even more incomplete than in the past, because State Capitalism carries with it the collapse of parliaments as a real governing force.

The trend of recent years emphasizes the fact of parliamentary impotence, and State Capitalism strengthens this trend. As government more and more adapts itself to the requirements of regulation of industry, the parliament breaks down in trying to cope with the new problems. The constituent and geographical basis of parliamentary government disqualifies it from performing industrial functions. The complexity of forces expressed in State Capitalism, independent of the necessity of a centralized autocracy in the struggles of Imperialism, renders parliamentary control futile and demoralizing. [6] The powers of the state centralize in the administration, while formally they may remain legislative. The regulation of industry becoming the dominant function of the state, experts and extra-parliamentary commissions are put in charge of this function of regulation, responsible to the administrative power, and not to the parliament. Parliaments may talk, but they do not act; they have no real control over events and the functions of government, becoming convenient forms for maintaining the illusion of democracy. This tendency toward an administrative autocracy is strengthened by the belligerent character of Imperialism, but fundamentally it is an expression of the industrial facts of State Capitalism, and necessary even if military considerations were excluded.

The capitalist state must not be strengthened but weakened by Socialist parliamentary criticism and action; the state must be undermined and dragged down by the developing class power and struggles of the proletariat by all the general means of action at its disposal.

Parliamentarism showed itself utterly futile in the European crisis, except in the revolutionary criticism of a few rebels such as Liebnecht, Rühle, and Morgari. The supreme utility attached to parliamentarism was a strong factor in destroying the morale and taming the fighting energy of Socialism. Even had the Socialists had the will to organize actual opposition to the war, what could they have done? Parliament had no real control over events; all the Socialist parliamentarians could have done was to vote against the war credits. The unions had no initiative, the parliamentary movement having always played the dominant role. A General Strike? But a General Strike implies a conscious and virile industrial proletariat and organization, aware of its power and accustomed to act without being subservient to a parliamentary and bureaucracy. The Social Democracy had always conceived the unions as an auxiliary of minor importance, denying them any decisive function. Moreover, the dominant unions had become imperialistic. The actual sources of power were centralized in an administrative autocracy, and only revolutionary mass action could have undermined these powers, – that general mass action out of which revolutionary struggles arise, but which was bitterly opposed by parliamentary, petty bourgeois Socialism.

151

Parliamentarism may become an expression of proletarian class power: it can never become class power itself.

As an expression of the general struggles of the proletariat, as a means of developing proletarian consciousness, as an integral phase of proletarian struggle as a whole, parliamentarism is necessary and of value. But it must relate itself to other forms of struggle; it must abandon the policy of social-reformism. The revolutionary Socialist does not abandon the struggle for immediate demands to the opportunist; on the contrary, the final and only answer to the misleading "immediate demands" of the opportunist is for the revolutionary Socialist to concentrate on immediate demands that imply an aggressive struggle against Capitalism and that are phases of the developing Social Revolution.

The revolutionary proletariat and Socialism, accordingly, organize against State Capitalism, against the bourgeois state and parliamentary government, preparing to substitute in their place an industrial, communist administration by and of the proletariat.

Footnotes

1. The growth of state ownership in Europe and the complete lack of any developing Socialism, compelled a pondering of the problem. In a lecture on *Socialism versus the State* (reprinted in the **New Review**, August 1914), Emile Vandervelde, prominent opportunist and now a social-patriot, said: "We see, with Guesde, as with Marx and Engels, that there is no confusion possible between Socialism and state ownership. They will have nothing to do with the capitalist state, except to fight it. If they wish to master it, it is only that they may abolish it. At most, they would use it during a transitory period of working class dictatorship." The latter statement is untrue; Marx recognized, and the proletarian revolution in Russia confirms the fact, that the proletariat cannot seize hold of the bourgeois state and use it for purposes of the revolution; the state is destroyed, and the dictatorship of the proletariat functions through a new "state," as in the Soviets, which is simply the organized workers and peasants, and

no other class in society.

2. President Wilson, during the early days of his first administration, used the phrase, "The Constitution of Peace," as covering a policy of class harmony. The harmony did not materialize; it was during this administration that the bloody struggles occurred at Ludlow, the Mesaba Range, and Passaic through strikes crushed ruhlessly by armed force. Moreover, not even the President's declarations against Big Capital were put into practice; the administration was compelled to accept the fact of the dominance of Big Capital, the basic factor in any program of State Capitalism.

3. Capitalism is the last expression of Class Rule. The economic foundation of Class Rule is the private ownership of the necessaries for production. The Social structure, or garb, of Class Rule is the political State – that social structure in which Government is an organ separate and apart from production, with no vital function other than the maintenance of the supremacy of the ruling class. The overthrow of Class Rule means the overthrow of the political State, and its substitution with the Industrial Social Order, under which the necessaries for production are collectively owned and operated by and for all the people ... Industrial Unionism is clear upon the goal – the substitution of the political State with the Industrial Government ... While Class Rule casts the nation, and, with the nation, its government, in the mold of territory, Industrial Unionism casts the nation in the mold of useful occupations, and transforms the nation's government into the representations from these ... Industrial Unionism is the Socialist Republic in the making; and the goal once reached, the Industrial Union is the Socialist Republic in operation. – Daniel De Leon, **Industrial Unionism**.

4. Scheme after scheme is being tried by the capitalist class to insure a satisfied and subject class of workers. Profit-sharing, welfare work, and other schemes having proven miserable failures, and democracy nor being the slogan of the day, "industrial democracy" is being used instead. As political democracy is simply a form of authority of the bourgeoisie over the workers, so this "industrial democracy" perpetuates the authority of the employers over the workers. This "industrial democracy" assumes the grandiloquent iorm of a "republic of labor." And, peculiarly, this "republic" is being introduced by the Rockefeller interests, which ruthlessly refuse to tolerate unionism or any independent action of the workers. The "republic" will be

introduced in the plants of the Standard Oil Co. of New Jersey on April 1. It means that the workers will select, by secret ballot, a committee of their own number "who will treat with the directors of the company in all matters concerning health, conditions, wages and situation of labor." The **New York Mail** says: "While in the last analysis the plan fails to give the men real control over their own working conditions, it has been tried in Colorado with success and has given the men there a practical labor government, maintained by themselves." And: "In Colorado, once the scene of labor troubles of magnitude, the Standard Oil Companies have found the new plan has assured a co-operation which has almost automatically ended serious disputes." The "republic of labor" leaves the workers a disorganized mass, wasting their energy in the election of committees and making recommendations which the directors don't have to accept. It cannot and will not end the struggle between labor and capital. At the best, it will simply increase the privileges of a small group of skilled workers as against the great mass of the unskilled. The only republic of labor that the proletariat will consider is an industrial communism organized and managed through the industrially organized producers, functioning in a new Socialist state that will supplant the bourgeois political state. – Louis C. Fraina, *The Republic of Labor,* **The New International**, April 1918.

5. The climax of this emasculation of Socialist political action was reached at the Indianapolis convention of the Socialist Party, which, in the notorious Section 6, Article II, defined political action as "participation in elections for public office and practical legislative and administrative work along the lines of the Socialist Party platform." This utterly reactionary and unscientific measure was repealed at the St. Louis Convention in 1917, but the practice and policy it defines have not yet in practice been completely repealed.

6. Our governmental machinery – city, state and national – is not geared to deal with serious economic problems. It breaks down when a demand is made on it for aid in regulating big economic forces. It does not know how to compel economic and social efficiency. – **New York Tribune**, February 25, 1917. Moreover, the arch-Imperialist London **Times** recently proposed, as an after-the-war measure, the reconstruction of the House of Commons, favoring the abolition of political representation based on geographical divisions, and insisting upon elections by trades, industries and occupations. Of course, such

a reconstruction would proceed on a capitalistic basis.

Chapter XI
Unionism and Mass Action

THE working class, as every revolutionary class, passes through a process of material and ideological development, in which its purposes and tactics, determined by the prevailing historical conditions, are transformed and adapted to new circumstances as they arise. This development, roughly, consists of three phases:

1. Isolated economic action, through craft unions and sporadic strikes, with a gradual development of the idea of independent political action as a revolutionary means of struggle.
2. Political action, in its parliamentary sense, dominant in the proletarian class movement, becomes conservative and incompatible with the development of the proletariat, does not adapt itself to this development; and revolutionary movements arise, industrial in character, that repudiate all politics.
3. The third phase, the phase into which we are now emerging, adjusts itself to new circumstances and the increasing development of the proletariat, recognizing industrial and political action as synthetic factors in the general mass action of the proletariat as phases of the dynamic struggles of the new social revolutionary era.

The proletariat steps upon the stage of history as a revolutionary class. It was the still immature class of workers that saved the French Revolution, that established a bourgeois revolution in spite of the cowardly hesitancy and compromise of the bourgeoisie. In all subsequent revolutions in France – and France is the classical exemplar of this period in the development of the proletariat – the workers were a dynamic factor; they made the revolution, but they could not retain control because of the immaturity of their class development. The great struggle of the Paris Commune was the final heroic act of this period, and at the same time a projection of what was to come. In the historical sense, these revolts were not revolution but insurrections, revivals of the action of the bourgeois revolution and dominated largely by its ideology. With the downfall of the Commune and the collapse of the social-revolutionary First International, the workers enter upon a new period, the period of systematic, peaceful organization and struggle, along national and moderate lines, and not international and revolutionary. The value of these early revolts lay in impressing the workers with a sense of their own class immaturity and driving out of their consciousness the surviving ideology of the bourgeois revolution.

The workers, when they organize against Capitalism, organize into unions to carry on a struggle for more wages and better conditions of work generally. Largely because their skill is still an important factor, (and these early movements are dominantly movements of skilled labor), the workers win certain concessions. But because they are skilled workers, and equally because Capitalism has not yet integrated industry and the proletariat, these movements do not assume revolutionary proportions, nor do they actually conquer material concessions. The economic action is isolated; there is no general contact of the working class with the capitalist class, and the conception of a more general class struggle arises, developing into politics and parliamentary activity. Through the action of politics, the workers oppose a general struggle to Capitalism, a struggle that cannot develop out of isolated economic action. At this period the concept of the workers engaging in independent class politics is revolutionary, as it develops the consciousness of class and establishes class contact with the ruling class.

Socialism, with its program of class politics, offers the workers a class conception and class activity that are historically revolutionary. This development marks an epoch in the proletarian movement. It arouses, ideologically and potentially at least, the workers' consciousness of class; and without this consciousness of class the proletariat is doomed either to futile insurrection or being an instrument for the promotion of rival bourgeois interests.

Accordingly, Socialism develops along the lines of politics, in the parliamentary sense. But a means of action may be revolutionary or conservative according to historical conditions and requirements. At one period, a particular means may be revolutionary; at another, considering new conditions which require new or supplementary means of action, it may become conservative, even reactionary. This is precisely what happens to Socialism in its parliamentary phase, which is its dominant phase. Where previously Socialism developed the consciousness of class and potential revolution in the proletariat, within the limits of its maturity, it now becomes a force that hampers this development.

Socialism in its early activity as a general organized movement was compelled to emphasize the action of politics because of the immaturity of the proletariat. The workers are scattered, and their struggles are largely directed against the individual employer; large scale industry has not developed sufficiently to make large masses of workers engage in a general industrial class struggle against Capitalism and the state. The workers, subjectively and objectively, find it difficult to establish general class contact with each other industrially; it could be, and it was, done through political contact of isolated workers. Socialism, the dominant parliamentary Socialism, sees in the unions simply a transitory phase which may be necessary under given conditions, but which are unimportant in comparison with politics, as is mass action and extra-parliamentary action generally. The unions are conceived as conservative instruments, as organizations that in fact retard the revolutionary development of the workers, – which is true, in the period under consideration, but not as an ultimate proposition. Socialism makes a fetish of politics; parliamentarism is emphasized as the instrument with which the proletariat may emancipate itself. But that happens which differs from the earlier Socialist politics; under the impulse of the national bias, social-reformism and an opportunism that refuses to adapt itself to new requirements, the parliamentary, as well as the general, activity of Socialism becomes conservative, hesitant, compromising. The dominant Socialism becomes a fetter upon the emancipation of the proletariat. [1]

This result does not arise out of any one fact, but out of a series of facts, previously considered; the central fact is that Socialism did not adjust itself to the development of the proletariat, nor to the social-revolutionary era objectively introduced by Imperialism and the war; and this failure to adjust purposes and tactics to the new proletarian and social conditions conservatizes Socialism, turns it into a reactionary force, – temporarily, to be sure, but still reactionary.

The concentration of industry and technological development generally have during the past twenty years revolutionized the material existence of the proletariat. On the one hand has been produced the typical proletarian of average unskilled labor; on the other, the integration of industry in mammoth proportions has developed the conditions for general class action of the workers through industrial means directed against the capitalist, not as an individual but as a class, and against the whole bourgeois regime and its state. The proletariat has been centralized into large industrial groupings, and its revolts and action constitute a general action against Capitalism, the tremors of which are felt throughout the whole industrial and social system. This development, coincident, it must be emphasized, with the rise of Imperialism, arouses discontent and revolts in the craft unions, which are unable to cope with the new developments, and in which the unskilled become a more and more influential factor. But even more significant are the great strikes involving large masses of unorganized unskilled workers, strikes that shake the very fabric of capitalist society, and the influence of which stimulate revolutionary currents within the Socialist organizations. Instead of recognizing the revolutionary vitality of these new developments, the dominant Socialism tries to compress and stultify them within the limits of the old tactics, tries to maintain the ascendancy of a Socialism expressing the non-revolutionary elements of skilled labor and the petty bourgeoisie. In its struggles against Capitalism and the dominant Socialism the unskilled industrial proletariat turns to mass action, a mass action that emphasizes the futility and reactionary character of pure and simple parliamentarism. [2]

The reactionary character of the dominant Socialism is expressed not simply in the failure to accept the new developments, but in the fact that it has frequently condemned and opposed manifestations of the new proletarian action, occasionally even actively betrayed the unskilled proletariat while it was in the midst of gigantic struggles against Capitalism.

The dominant Socialism maintains its influence because of prestige, the conservatism of organization, and the insufficiently developed consciousness of the unskilled proletariat; but it is gradually undermined by industrial development and its new requirements. The industrial proletariat is "organized by the very mechanism of capitalist production itself;" industry becomes co-ordinated, integrated, and the strikes of the unskilled workers assume revolutionary significance, antagonizing the dominant craft unions and parliamentary Socialism, and striking directly at Capitalism through the industrial source of capitalist .supremacy. While antagonisms between the *bloc* of skilled labor and the *petite bourgeoisie* as against the capitalist class are softened, the antagonisms between le industrial proletariat and Capitalism are sharpened. Industrial struggles become more and more general, larger in scope and intensity; a new epoch of class war emerges, relentless in spirit and aggressive in purpose, – a class war having as its driving force the mass action of the industrial proletariat of average labor.

The new conditions of proletarian struggle develop new conceptions and organization, or ideas of organization. The facts of industrial concentration, the decreasing importance of skilled labor, the massing of industrial control in a centralized capitalist autocracy, gender more and more futile the economic struggles of the craft unions, which now engage largely in industrial and political bargaining. But a new and militant force arises in the unions, composed of the unskilled and those whose skill has been expropriated by the machine process; revolutionary currents develop, and the problem of industrial unionism becomes an issue. Industrial unionism, however, is incompatible with the dominant forces in the craft unions; the unskilled are a minority, and industrial unionism is turned into a compromise, a grotesque compromise in the form of "amalgamations." The concept of industrial unity and solidarity of action cannot break through the pride and prestige of craft and property; industrial unionism founders on the rocks of craft disputes and jurisdictional squabbles, which absorb so much of craft union activity. The craft unions are completely destroyed, as in the steel industry, or they become, largely, mere "job trusts" and instruments of peaceful bargaining and compromise with the employers, supplemented by betrayals of the unskilled.

Industrial unionism becomes an expression of, and develops real strength and influence among, the unskilled workers, in whom common conditions of labor; absence of craft distinctions and the discipline of machine industry develop the necessity and potentiality of the industrial form of organization. [3] The power of this proletariat lies in its mass and numbers, in its lack of artificial distinctions of skill and craft. Being a product of the massing of workers in a particular industry, the unskilled strike *en masse*, act through mass action; being united and disciplined by concentrated industry and its machine process, the unskilled proletariat organizes its unions industrially, in accord with the facts of industry, in accord with the conditions of its work and existence. Industrial unionism in form is an expression of the integration of industry and the proletariat by the mechanism of capitalist production itself, and it becomes peculiarly the unionism of the revolutionary proletariat. All groups of workers in an industry are organized and unified into one union, "cast in the mold of the industry in which they work, artificial differences of occupational divisions being swept aside. Strikes become general and acquire political significance, action becomes the action of the mass, the integrated action of an integrated proletariat. Where the craft unions initiated the strike of a single group of workers in an industry, the industrial union initiates a strike of *all the workers*. The ideology of solidarity becomes the practice of solidarity.

Industrial unionism, as the expression of unskilled workers impelled by objective conditions to subjectively accept class action, acquires a revolutionary concept, consciousness and activity. Instead of the craft union motto of "A fair day's pay for a fail day's work," industrial unionism inscribes upon its banners the revolutionary motto, "Abolition of the wages system." The ultimate purpose of industrial. unionism is the organization of all the workers in accord with the facts of production, constructing in this way the structure of the new society within the old, as a necessary phase in the overthrow of Capitalism and the establishment of a new society which shall function through the industrially organized producers. Not the state, but the industrial union is the instrument of revolution, – equally the might for the revolutionary act and the norm of the new society. Industrial unionism is not simply a means, a more effective means than any previously used, to carry on the every-day struggle against the employing class: it is Socialism in action and Socialism in the making. [4]

But the dominant conservative Socialism refuses to accept, it cannot accept unless transforming itself, the revolutionary implications of industrial unionism. Organized Socialism persists in rendering stultifying homage to the fetish of parliamentarism. The general defects of parliamentarism are emphasized and multiplied by the conditions of State Capitalism and the developing requirements of the proletariat of average labor: it cannot express the requirements of this proletariat, nor can it successfully wage the struggle against

State Capitalism, which means an intensification of class antagonisms and struggles and the development of an emerging proletarian state through industrial unions as against the state of imperialistic State Capitalism. The new movements of the industrial proletariat engage in a struggle to revolutionize the dominant Socialism; the struggle fails and is relinquished, developing the idea that Socialist politics *as such* are not and never can become revolutionary; the trend becomes one of severing relations with Socialism, and the revolutionary movements of the proletariat acquire an active or passive non-political bias. This development emphasizes the vital defects of the parliamentary policy of Socialism. [5]

This non-political policy is temporary, being the product of transitory conditions. As industrial unionism engages more and more in the general class fight against Capitalism, as parliamentary Socialism weakens under the pressure of revolutionary events, each in itself and even jointly are considered incomplete, and the two means of action become merged in the general action of the proletariat, centralized, dominated and energized by revolutionary mass action.

What are the limitations of industrial unionism and parliamentary action in their particularized activity?

Parliamentary action in and of itself cannot realize the militant independence of the proletariat, marshal its forces and organize its revolutionary action. Parliamentary activity is an expression of the proletarian struggle, not the struggle itself; it is a form of expression of class power., but not a fundamental factor in developing this class power. Parliamentarism in itself cannot alter the actual bases of power in the class struggle, nor develop that force without which the aspirations of the Revolution are unrealizable. All propaganda, all electoral and parliamentary activity are insufficient for the overthrow of Capitalism,impotent when the ultimate test of the class struggle turns into a test of *power*. The power for the Social Revolution issues out of the actual struggles of the proletariat, out of its strikes, its industrial unions and mass action. The peaceful parliamentary conquest of the state is either sheer utopia or reaction; this conception forgets two important things: the actual power of government resides in industry and in an administrative autocracy, not in parliaments, and this power, must he overthrown by extra parliamentary action; while it is utterly inconceivable that revolutionary Socialism should ever secure power through an electoral majority under the forms of bourgeois democracy. Parliamentarism is actually counter-revolutionary, as it strengthens the fetish of democracy: bourgeois democracy must be annihilated before the proletarian revolution may function. The revolution is an act of a minority, at first; of the most class conscious section of the industrial proletariat, which, in a test of electoral strength, would be a minority, but which, being a solid, industrially indispensable class, can disperse and defeat all other classes through the annihilation of the fraudulent democracy of the parliamentary system implied in the dictatorship of the proletariat, imposed upon society by means of revolutionary mass action.

State capitalism, through it weakening of parliamentary control and its centralized administrative autocracy, emphasizes the insufficiency of parliamentarism. But yet the proletarian, movement cannot reject politics. Paradoxical though it may appear, State Capitalism, while it emphasizes the futility of parliamentarism in and of itself, broadens the scope and necessity of politics. In unifying ruling class interests and imposing a drastic regulation upon industry, State Capitalism makes the state a vital issue of the class struggle in its general aspects. More and more the state concerns itself directly in industrial disputes: the class struggle becomes intensely political. Politics is the field in which all issues of the class struggle are in action. It is not a single issue, but the totality of issues arising out of the antagonisms of bourgeois society that the proletariat must struggle against. It is not through ownership of industry alone that the capitalist maintains his rule; the simple fact of ownership is itself maintained by a large number of means, a large number of issues, social, political, international, – all of which are centralized in State Capitalism. The proletariat must interest itself in all these issues, engage in the parliamentary struggle through which capitalist society as a whole stands forth naked and unashamed.

The parliamentary struggle, waged in a revolutionary spirit and as a phase of the general action of the proletariat, issues a challenge to capitalist supremacy in every issue that comes up for discussion, the totality of issues which insures bourgeois supremacy. It is not through securing better wages and better conditions of labor that the proletariat conquers social power, but by weakening Capitalism in all the issues that maintain its ascendancy. Parliamentary action centers attention on all these issues; if revolutionary, parliamentary action realizes the futility, however, of solving these issues through politics alone, and it therefore calls to the struggle the industrial and mass action of the proletariat in class political strikes. This unity of means and action develops class consciousness and class power. By concentrating on all issues that are vital to Capitalism, revolutionary Socialist parliamentarism emphasizes and intensifies the antagonism between proletariat and bourgeoisie, and in this sense awakens the consciousness and general action of the proletariat. At one moment, politics develop into industrial and mass action; at another moment, these develop into politics: the two are inseparable phases of the same dynamic process of class action, each dependent upon and developing the other. Socialist parliamentarism, accordingly, should not be an empty means of protest or a futile means of "democratizing" the state and "growing into" Socialism, but a dynamic phase of proletarian action; and, recognizing its limitations and utility, becomes a supreme method of developing revolutionary and class consciousness ideologically, which is transformed into class power by industrial and mass action.

Industrial unionism, in itself , and even if it recognizes and accepts the Socialist parliamentary struggle, has its own limitations. Industrial unionism, in its dogmatic expression, assumes a general organization of the proletariat before Socialism can be established, the construction of a general industrial organization that may seize and operate industry. In terms of infinity, it may be conceivable that some day, some how, toe majority of the proletariat, or an overwhelming minority, may become organized into industrial unions under Capitalism. In terms of actual practice, this is inconceivable. The proletariat of unskilled labor, which alone may accept industrial unionism, is a class difficult to organize; its conditions of labor discourage organization and make it move and act under the impulse of mass action. The conditions of Capitalism, its violent upheavals and stress of struggle, exclude the probability of an all-inclusive proletarian organization; moreover, should we hesitate to act until this general organization materializes [6], Capitalism may turn in on itself and establish a new form of slavery. In its dogmatic expression, industrial unionism has much in common with the parliamentary Socialist conception of the peaceful "growing into" Socialism; it evades the dynamic problems of the Revolution, substituting theory for reality and formula for action. It is fantastic as a general proposition, it is particularly fantastic considering the period of violent upheavals and struggle into which the world is now emerging, to consider that the proletariat under Capitalism can through industrialism organize the structure of the new society. The structure of industrialism, the form of the new communist society, can be organized only during the transition period from Capitalism to Socialism acting through the dictatorship of the proletariat; all that can be done in the meanwhile is to develop a measure of industrial organization and its ideology of the industrial state, which may constitute the starting point for a proletarian dictatorship in its task of introducing the industrial state of communist Socialism.

The supremacy of the proletariat is determined by its action, and not by its organization. The proletariat acts even where there is no organization, through mass action; organization is a means to action, and not a substitute for action. The function of an organization, in the revolutionary sense, is that it may serve as the centre for action of the unorganized proletarian masses, rally and integrate the general mass action of the proletariat, organizing and directing it for the conquest of power. Socialism hastens the overthrow of Capitalism through revolutionary action. In this sense, parliamentarism and industrial unionism become integral phases of mass action.

Mass action is not a *form* of action as much as it is a *process and synthesis* of action. [7] It is the unity of all forms of proletarian action, a means of throwing the proletariat, organized and unorganized, in a general struggle against Capitalism and the capitalist state. It is the sharp, definite expression of the revolt of the workers under the impact of the antagonisms and repressions of Capitalism, of the recurring crises and revolutionary situations produced by the violent era of Imperialism. Mass action is the instinctive action of the proletariat, gradually developing more conscious and organized forms and definite purposes. It is extra-parliamentary in method, although political;in purpose and result, may develop into and be itself developed by the parliamentary struggle.

Organizations, political and economic, have a tendency to become conservative; a tendency emphasized, moreover, by the fact that they largely represent the more favored groups of workers. These organizations must be swept out of their conservatism by the elemental impact of mass action, functioning through organized and unorganized workers acting instinctively under the pressure of events and in disregard of bureaucratic discipline. The great expressions of mass action in recent years, the New Zealand General Strike, the Lawrence strike, the great strike of the British miners under which capitalist society reeled on the verge of collapse, – all were mass actions organized and carried through in spite of the passive and active hostility of the dominant Socialist and labor organizations, under the impulse of mass action, the industrial proletariat senses its own power and acquires the force to act equally against Capitalism and the conservatism of organizations. Indeed, a vital feature of mass action is precisely that it places in the hands of the proletariat the power to overcome the fetters of these organizations, to act in spite of their conservatism, and through proletarian mass action emphasize antagonisms between workers and capitalists, and conquer power. A determining phase of the proletarian revolution in Russia was its acting against the dominant Socialist organization, sweeping these aside through its mass action before it could seize social supremacy. And the great strikes and demonstrations in Germany and Austria during February 1918, potentially revolutionary in character, were a form of mass action that broke loose against the open opposition of the dominant Socialist and union organizations, and that were crushed by this opposition. *Mass action is the proletariat itself in action*, dispensing with bureaucrats and intellectuals acting through its own initiative; and it is precisely this circumstance that horrifies the soul of petty bourgeois Socialism. The masses are to act upon their own initiative and the impulse of their own struggles; it is the function of the revolutionary Socialist to provide the program and the course for this elemental action, to adapt himself to the new proletarian modes of struggle.

Mass action organizes and develops into the political strike and demonstration, in which a general political issue is the source of the action. Political mass action is determined not by the struggle for wages, but by general issues of prime political importance, in which the proletariat centralizes and integrates its forces, in which organized and unorganized workers may act together in a general struggle against Capitalism. This concentration of forces through mass action is an indispensable condition for the general revolutionary struggles in the days to come.

Mass action may consist of a spontaneous strike of organized workers in revolt against the union bureaucracy; or, as is most usually the case, of the strikes and action of unorganized, just skilled workers. These are primitive forms of mass action, although they constitute the genesis of the general mass action which may include workers, organized and unorganized, in various industrial groupings, in a sweeping struggle against Capitalism on general class issues. An important fact, a fact that disposes of the cheap sneers of petty bourgeois Socialism stigmatizing these manifestations as "anarchistic" and "slum proletarian," is that these mass actions are an expression of the industrial proletariat against the centralized industry of dominant Capitalism. The mass that functions through mass action is the industrial proletarian mass, the cohesive action of which may attract other social groups to the great struggle.

As an historic process, mass action is an expression and recognition of the fact that the new era is an era of violent struggles, of an acute crisis of antagonisms, of the impact of the proletariat in a revolutionary situation against Capitalism for the definite revolutionary conquest of power.

Imperialistic State Capitalism, while trying to and temporarily succeeding in softening antagonisms, actually and fundamentally multiplies the antagonisms and contradictions inherent in Capitalism. These antagonisms assume a violent form, equally between nations, and between the proletariat and the bourgeoisie. This crisis in antagonisms constitutes the social-revolutionary era, in which the proletariat is driven to violent struggles against Capitalism through mass action. The social-revolutionary era finds its expression and its tactic in mass action: this is the great fact of contemporary proletarian development.

The process of revolution consists in a weakening of the class power of the bourgeoisie as against a strengthening of the class power of the proletariat. The class power of the proletariat arises out of the intensity of its struggles and revolutionary energy. It consists, moreover, of undermining the bases of the power and morale of the capitalist state, a process that requires extra-parliamentary activity through mass action. Capitalism trembles when it meets the impact of a strike in a basic industry; Capitalism will more than tremble, it will actually verge on a collapse, when it meets the impact of a general mass action involving a number of correlated industries, and developing into revolutionary mass action against the whole capitalist regime. The value of this mass action is that it shows the proletariat its power, weakens Capitalism, and compels the state largely to depend upon the use of brutal force in the struggle, either the physical force of the military or the force of legal terrorism; this emphasizes antagonisms between proletarian and capitalist, widening the scope and deepening the intensity of the proletarian struggle against Capitalism. General mass action, moreover, a product of the industrial proletariat, will, by the impulse and psychology of events and the emphasizing of antagonisms, draw within the orbit of the struggle workers still under the control of the craft unions. Mass action, being the proletariat itself in action, loosens its energy, develops enthusiasm, and unifies the action of the workers to its utmost measure.

It is this concentration of proletarian forces that makes mass action the method of the proletarian revolution. It is this dynamic quality of mass action that makes it the expression of an era in which the proletariat throws itself in violent struggles against Capitalism. The proletarian revolution is a test of power, a process of forcible struggles, an epoch in which the proletariat requires a flexible method of action, a method of action that will not only concentrate all its available forces, but which will develop its initiative and consciousness, allowing it to seize and use any particular means of struggle in accord with a prevailing situation and necessary under the conditions.

Moreover, mass action means the repudiation of bourgeois democracy. Socialism will come not through the peaceful, democratic parliamentary conquest of the state, but through the determined and revolutionary mass action of a proletarian minority. The fetish of democracy is a fetter upon the proletarian revolution; mass action smashes the fetish, emphasizing that the proletariat recognizes no limits to its action except the limits of its own power. The proletariat will never conquer unless it proceeds to struggle after struggle; its power is developed and its energy let loose only through action. Parliamentarism, in and of itself, fetters proletarian action; organizations are often equally fetters upon action; the proletariat must act and always act: through action it conquers. The great merit and necessity of mass action is that it frees the energy, while it co-ordinates the forces, of the proletariat, compels the proletariat to act uncompromisingly and reject the "rights" of any other class; and action destroys hesitancy and a faltering with the revolutionary task. [8]

The great war has objectively brought Europe to the verge of revolt. Capitalist society at any moment may be thrust into the air by an upheaval of the proletariat, – as in Russia. Whence will the impulse for the revolutionary struggle come? Surely not from the moderate Socialism and unionism, which are united solidly in favor of an imperialistic war; surely not from futile parliamentary rhetoric, even should it be revolutionary rhetoric. The impulse will come out of the mass action of the proletariat, and it is this mass action alone that can sweep aside the hesitancy and the risks, that can topple over the repressions and power of the bourgeois state. Mass action is the dynamic impulse of the revolutionary proletarian struggle, whatever the specific form it may assume; in the actual revolutionary period, mass action unites all forms of struggle in one sweeping action against Capitalism, each contributing its share as integral phases of the general mass action, – as in the proletarian revolution in Russia. In a crisis, the state rigidly controls all the available forces of normal action; parliaments become impotent, and a "state of siege" prevails that can be broken through only by revolutionary mass action, – equally during war and in any revolutionary situation.

Mass action is dynamic, pliable, creative; the proletariat

through mass action instinctively adapts itself to the means and tactics necessary in a prevailing situation. The forms of activity of the proletariat are not limited and stultified by mass action, they are broadened, deepened and co-ordinated. Mass action is, equally a process of revolution and the Revolution itself in operation.

Footnotes

1. Just as the national states became an obstacle to the development of the forces of production, so the Socialist parties became the chief obstacle to the development of the revolutionary movements of the working class. – Leon Trotzky, The War and the International.

2. "The caute of the new tactical differences," says Anton Pannekoek, "arises from the fact that under the influence of the modern form of capitalism the labor movement lias taken on a new form of action, to wit, mass action;" and in criticizing Kautsky, to whom the new tactics appear as anarchistic, Pannekoek says, "for Kautsky mass action is an act of revolution, for us it is a process of revolution."

3. In this country, the history of the Industrial Workers of the World proves conclusively that industrial unionism is a movement of the proletariat of unskilled labor. The convention that organized the IWW in 1905 consisted of skilled and unskilled, but the skilled workers gradually deserted the organization; and the real history and significance of the IWW has been precisely its expressing the developing consciousness and action of the unskilled workers. It is this circumstance that made the IWW a revolutionary portent in the labor movement. The non-recognition of this fact was largely responsible for the violent attacks made upon the IWW as organized after 1908, by Daniel De Leon and the Socialist Labor Party; and this fact also is responsible for the antagonism and often open warfare between the IWW and the dominant forces in the Socialist Party.

4. Karl Kautsky, who usually sees clearly in theory but hesitates and compromises miserably in practice, an attitude typical of the "centrist," said in an article in the International Socialist Review, April 1901: "The trades unions ... will constitute the most energetic factors in surmounting the present mode of production and they will

be pillars on which the edifice of the Socialist commonwealth will be erected." This is a recognition of the revolutionary mission of unionism. But the trades unions are not working for the revolution; they are working for a place in the governing system of things, – making for State Capitalism, and not Socialism. Nor does the structure of the trades unions admit of their waging a revolutionary struggle against Capitalism or of assuming management of concentrated industry.

5. The conquest of political supremacy becomes a peaceful process, which so far as the masses are concerned consists only of propaganda and elections. It is the work of the Social Democracy *as a political party*; other working class organizations, even the labor unions, are unnecessary ... The defect of pure and simple parliamentarism lies in the fact that it considers the form of suffrage as something absolute and independent. But precisely like the entire constitution the suffrage is merely an expression of the *actual relations of power* in society ... The peaceful parliamentary conquest of power ... pre-supposes universal suffrage, and universal suffrage can simply be abolished by a parliament. – Anton Pannekoek, *Socialism and Labor Unionism*, in The New Review, July 1913.

6. A general organization of the workers will always remain impossible under Capitalism because of its continuous state of development. – H. Lauffenberg, The Political Strike, 1914.

7. Rosa Luxemburg has called the mass strike the dynamic method of the proletarian masses, the characteristic form of the proletarian struggle in the Revolution. She considers mass action, and its most important feature, the mass strike, as the sum total of a period in the class struggle that may last for years and tens of years until victory comes to the proletariat. In permanent change, it comprises all phases of the political and economic struggle, all phases of the. Revolution. Mass action, in its highest form of political strike, means the unity of political and economic action, means the proletarian revolution as a historic process" ... If industrial action is the most efficient form of mass action, why bother about minor issues? Why not concentrate all our efforts and thought in building our industrial unions so strong as to overcome the capitalist employer and the capitalist state? Such an objection overlooks the complexity of real conditions. We are not free to choose our methods in accordance with certain theoretical constructions, but have to build on the solid ground of actual facts in

174

the light of historical developments ... Industrial organization has its historical limits beyond which we cannot rise at the given moment of our action. Large groups of workers will continue for a certain length of time to organize in craft unions, and although we will tell them they are wrong, and fight them where injurious to their class, still they will be a factor in our revolutionary struggle, either for or against ... We are convinced that the technical development of the capitalist world makes conditions ripe for the Socialist commonwealth at this very moment, that only our lack of power stands in the way of the realization of our hopes. What we want above all is a unity and concentration of the forces already existing in a latent form, a combination and further development of these forces towards our revolutionary aims. – S.J. Rutgers, *Mass Action and Socialism*, The New International, February 1918.

8. The Council [of Workers and Soldiers, during the earlier period of the Russian Revolution, when the Menshevik and Social-Revolutionist moderates were in control] hesitates; and out of hesitancy conies compromise. It imagines that the course of the Revolution may be determined by interminable discussions among the intellectuals: it acts only under pressure of the revolutionary masses. It talks revolution, while the government acts reaction. It takes refuge in proclamations, in discussion, in appeals to a pseudo-theory, in everything save the revolutionary action of the masses directed aggressively to a solution of the pressing problems of the day ... Where revolutions do not act immediately, particularly the proletarian revolution, reaction appears and controls the situation; and the formerly revolutionary representatives of the masses accept and strengthen this reaction. Once revolutionary ardor cools, the force of bourgeois institutions and control of industry weights the balance in favor of the ruling class. Revolutions march from action to action : action, more action, again action, supplemented by an audacity that shrinks at nothing, – these are the tactics of the proletarian revolution ... The Council hampers and tries to control the instincts and action of the masses, instead of directing them in a way that leaves the initiative to the masses – developing that action of the masses out of which class power arises ... Instead of action – phrases; instead of Revolution – a paltering with the revolutionary task ... Its failure to act accordingly marked the decline of its power and influence *as then constituted*: the task of the Council now became that of revolutionizing itself, of discarding its old policy and personnel.

And this revolutionary process could develop only out of the masses, not out of the Council's intellectual representatives: these representatives had to be thrust aside, brutally and contemptuously. – Louis C. Fraina, *The Proletarian Revolution in Russia*, The Class Struggle, January-February 1918.

Chapter XII
The Proletarian Revolution

THE theory of the gradual transformation of Capitalism into Socialism, of a peaceful "growing into" Socialism, depends upon two assumptions: the collectivism of State Capitalism is an approach to Socialism, that *will* gradually and of its own compulsion become transformed into Socialism; and State Capitalism, operating jointly with an enlightened and organized working class, will succeed in limiting and restraining the economic forces of Capitalism. Our analysis of actual facts and forces shows, however, that State Capitalism means Capitalism at the violent climax of its development, intensifying the subjection of the proletariat and the domination of the capitalist class. The economic forces of Capitalism have not been limited, they have burst forth in a violent upheaval, the most violent of the ages; and these forces will burst forth, in new upheavals unless directed into the channel of Social Revolution. Nor have the organizations of the workers succeeded in restraining the tendencies of Capitalism: the imperialistic Capitalism of Germany, France and Great Britain, in which operate powerful Socialist and labor organizations, have precipitated the proletariat and the world into a catastrophe the agony and oppression of which are inconceivable. If all this means a limiting of the forces of Capitalism and a "growing into" Socialism, then may heaven have mercy upon the world and the proletariat!

This theory often appears in pseudo-Marxian garb is, in fact, a distortion and a repudiation of Marxism.

Marxism conceives the Social Revolution as a dynamic process of proletarian struggles in a period when the forces of production in capitalist society come in conflict with the old relations of production, relations which develop into fetters upon the productive process. This conflict creates a social-revolutionary crisis, a revolutionary situation and a breach in

177

the old order in which the proletariat breaks through for action and the conquest of power. All the developments of bourgeois society simply produce the objective conditions for the proletarian revolution out of which emerges Socialism; these developments alone never can and won't bring Socialism. The process consists of two phases: the objective development of Capitalism and the subjective development of the proletariat. Historically these two phases of the process are one; actually, they are not necessarily a unity: Germany, with an intense development of Capitalism and an apparently mature proletariat, has not yet developed a proletarian revolution, in spite of the revolutionary activity of capitalistically inferior Russia.

The epoch of Imperialism, which means Capitalism at the climax of its development, meets the requirements of the Marxian analysis. All the violence, all the upheavals of Imperialism are symptoms of the revolt of Capitalism against the fetters placed upon the productive forces. The requirements of developing Capitalism are incompatible with the capitalist forms of production. The crisis is acute. Capitalism strives to break the fetters, annihilate the multiplying contradictions, through State Capitalism and Imperialism, only to strengthen the fetters and increase the contradictions, resulting in a mad, violent and destructive world war. The economic and social, the political and national bases of Capitalism are now fetters upon the forces of production: the fetters must be broken, they can be broken only by the Social Revolution; and Capitalism writhes in the agony of its struggles, a mad beast rending itself and the world. Imperialism, accordingly, introduces a new epoch in Capitalism, the social-revolutionary epoch. Objectively, a revolutionary situation prevails; subjectively, the proletariat must prepare itself for the final revolutionary struggle against Capitalism.

It is the tragedy of Imperialism that it can produce maggots only. It cannot, except temporarily, dispose of the contradictions implied in a fettering of the forces of production.

The imperialistic nation seeks to broaden the base of its economic activity through conquest and the development of new territory; but in accomplishing this, the base is correspondingly narrowed for other nations, and for the world. And even the imperialistically triumphant nation secures only momentary relief: the new territory is developed, and again there is a surplus of commodities and of capital, again the vicious circle of production of means of production for new commodity production; and again within the triumphant nation itself there is a crisis, supplemented by still more acute crises within the defeated nations. A new upheaval arises, new and more violent wars, new and more intense waste. War becomes the normal aspect of Imperialism.

There is no alternative for the proletariat: either war and again war, or the Social Revolution.

The world war has brought Capitalism to the verge of collapse. It has compelled the state to lay a dictatorial hand upon the process of production, and the nation to negate its own basis by striving to break through the limits of the nation. It has compelled industrial necessity to subordinate itself to the overwhelming fact of military necessity. The debts of the belligerent nations are colossal, and they will fetter the nations, constitute a crucial problem in the days to come. The war has weakened Capitalism while it has strengthened a fictitious domination of the capitalist class. Contradictions and antagonisms have been multiplied. War has become the normal occupation of Capitalism, and the transition to peace will shake Capitalism to its foundations, posing new and more acute problems for solution. Industry will have to adjust itself to a peace basis, and it will be a herculean task; the proletariat will have to adjust itself to the new conditions, new struggles and new problems, and the experiences of war are not calculated to make it submissive.

The proletariat will find upon the conclusion of peace that all its sacrifices have availed it naught, and that the old system of exploitation persists in intensified form. Capitalism will equally find that war has availed it naught: its old economic problems will not have been solved and new problems have been created. Will Capitalism answer with a feverish era of industrial expansion? But war debts will weigh upon the nation, and an era of expansion will simply hasten the new crisis and a new war. There is a point where Capitalism comes up against an impasse in the industrial process. The forces of production inexorably generate new contradictions and crises. Capitalism verges on collapse.

The fatalist uses these facts, and they *are* facts, as an argument for an inevitable collapse of Capitalism and an equally inevitable coming of Socialism. The argument is as futile as it is fatalistic. The world war, in which millions of workers have sacrificed and died in the cause of Imperialism, is a warning of an alternative. The fatalist attitude in practice allows Capitalism to dispose of things in its own brutal way. And instead of a coming of Socialism, the world may see the coming of a new barbarism, the "common ruin of the contending classes." If war becomes the normal state of society, if the proletariat as the modern revolutionary class has not the initiative and the energy to assume control of society, then instead of a new society we shall have a new era of rapine and conquest. Europe rending itself, Europe and America rending each other, and the two rending Asia, or Asia rending them all. A collapse of Capitalism, in one form or another, is inevitable; but the coming of Socialism is not equally inevitable. [1] It may become a collapse of all civilization.

What determined the supremacy of the bourgeoisie was its possession of actual material power, of the ownership of capital. It was a propertied class, and property as a class prerogative imparts power and ultimate ascendancy. The proletariat is a non-propertied, an expropriated class; what will determine its supremacy is revolutionary energy and integrity, and these alone.

180

The development during the war of Socialist social-reformism into social-Imperialism is an acute expression of a danger that besets the proletariat. Is it imaginary, is it inconceivable, in view of the unbelievable events in Europe, that the proletariat, instead of an instrument of revolution, might become an instrument of imperialistic conquest and spoliation? Only an uncompromising adherence to the revolutionary task, only the conscious and definite emergence of revolutionary Socialism, may avert the catastrophe. The subjective factor of a revolutionary proletariat alone will convert the objective conditions of Capitalism into Socialism. The proletariat will act, but its action must be directed. It may be skewed awry by petty bourgeois Socialism, as was unsuccessfully attempted in Russia and as was successfully done in Austria and Germany. The shortcomings of the dominant Socialism might convert proletarian action into a weapon of proletarian suicide. The tactics of petty bourgeois Socialism may not completely destroy the revolution, but they may hamper it and prolong the period of agony of imperialistic Capitalism.

In this epoch of Imperialism, of war and catastrophe, of actual and potential betrayals of the proletariat, the Socialist cannot swerve from the fundamentals of Socialism. Social-reformism means a paltering with the revolutionary task, social-Imperialism means a betrayal of the revolutionary task: and it is that way disaster lies. There are many dangers that beset the path of the proletariat, dangers that the Socialist must appreciate and guard against. The bourgeois revolution was, in a sense, automatic: its possession of property insured its ultimate supremacy. Indeed, the bourgeois revolution triumphed in spite of its cowardly hesitancy and vacillation, in spite of disastrous mistakes; its struggles were one long series of compromises with the feudal class, even on the verge of victory; and where the revolution was drastic and definite, as in France, it was because of the courage and action of the peasantry and the city proletarians. But mistakes may be fatal to the proletariat, because the proletariat is an expropriated class. The proletarian revolution is not in any sense of the word an automatic process: it will conquer only through uncompromising action, courageous and unrelenting adherence to the class struggle, and by developing the necessary clarity of understanding of the epoch we are in, an understanding that will avoid tactical mistakes and offer a definite, decisive program of revolutionary action to the proletariat.

The class character and independence of the revolution must be emphasized under any and all conditions; the proletariat must not be lured into compromises either with Capitalism or its own organizations, compromises that invade its class integrity and palsy its action. On with the struggle, in spite of all and everything! The epoch is an epoch of revolutionary, uncompromising struggle and this struggle alone shall prevail.

The process of proletarian struggles will, under the impact of antagonisms and a revolutionary situation, develop into the great and final struggle, – an intense, violent and uncompromising struggle against Capitalism. This struggle will not break out as a conscious, organized struggle for Socialism: it will break out under the impulse of a crisis, through mass action. Its character, of course, will initially vary in accord with prevailing conditions, although probably, at first, animated by petty or vague purposes. And its course will be determined by the sense of reality, consciousness of purpose and power of revolutionary Socialism, its capacity to propose and organize a revolutionary program around which the masses may rally for action and the conquest of power. Organizing and directing the revolution will become the supreme task of Socialism, a test equally of its uncompromising spirit and its sense of reality. The policy of revolutionary phrases is as disastrous as the policy of parliamentary rhetoric and dickering with the bourgeois state. Revolutions do not rally around dogmas, but programs; and the program of the proletarian revolution must be as practical and realistic as it is revolutionary and uncompromising. Reality and the revolution are one, united and made dynamic by the class character of the proposals and purposes of the proletariat in action.

The immediate objective of the proletarian revolution is the conquest of the power of the state and this means the annihilation of the bourgeois state, its parliamentary system and bourgeois democracy and the introduction of a new "state" comprised in the dictatorship of the proletariat. [2] In his **Criticism of the Gotha Program** Marx projected this phase of the proletarian revolution:

"Between the capitalist and the communist systems of society lies the period of the revolutionary transformation of the one into the other. This corresponds to a political transition period, whose state can be nothing else than the revolutionary dictatorship of the proletariat.!"

The alternative to this dictatorship of the proletariat is the bourgeois state, its democracy and parliamentary system. To compromise with this system is to yield up the revolutionary task and to allow Capitalism to dominate. The parliamentary bourgeois state must be destroyed not simply because it is the ultimate purpose of Socialism to do away with the state as constituted in bourgeois society, but because it is immediately necessary in the process of disposing of the old society and introducing the new. It is a tactical necessity. The dictatorship of the proletariat is a revolutionary recognition of the fact that the proletariat alone counts, and no other class has any "rights." The dictatorship of the proletariat places all power in the control of the proletariat, and weakens the bourgeoisie, makes them incapable of any concerted action against the Revolution. Organized in a dictatorship of the proletariat, the Revolution unhesitatingly and relentlessly pursues its task of reconstructing society on the basis of communist Socialism.

The parliamentary regime is the expression of bourgeois democracy, – each equally an instrument for the promotion of bourgeois class interests. Parliamentarism, presumably representing all classes, actually represents and promotes the requirements of the ruling class alone. Its trappings of army, police and judiciary are indispensable means of repression used against the proletariat, and the proletariat in action annihilates them all: in place of the army, the armed proletarian militia, until unnecessary; in place of the police, disciplinary measures of the masses themselves; in place of the judiciary, tribunals of workmen. The bureaucratic machinery of the state disappears. The division of functions in the parliamentary system into legislative and executive has for its direct purpose the indirect smothering of the opposition, the legislature talks and represents the pretense of "democracy," while the executive acts autocratically. The parliamentary system is a fetter upon revolutionary class action in the epoch of the ftoal struggle against Capitalism. The proletarian revolution annihilates the parliamentary system and its division of functions, legislative and executive being united in one body, – as in the Paris Commune and in the Russian Councils of Workers and Peasants.

The dictatorship of the proletariat, moreover, annihilates bourgeois democracy. All democracy is relative, is *class* democracy. As an historical category, democracy is a form of authority of one class over another; bourgeois democracy is the form of expression of the authority and tyranny of Capitalism. Authority is an instrument of class rule, historically: Socialism destroys authority. The democracy of Socialism, the self-government of the proletarian masses, discards the democracy of Capitalism relative democracy is superseded by the individual and social autonomy of communist Socialism. The proletarian revolution does not allow the "ethical concepts" of bourgeois democracy to interfere in the course of events: it ruthlessly sweeps aside "democracy" in the process of revolutionary transformation. Capitalism hypocritically insists upon a government of *all the classes*; the Revolution frankly and fearlessly introduces the government of *one class, the proletariat*, through a proletarian dictatorship. The proletarian revolution is inexorable; it completely and ruthlessly annihilates the institutions and ideology of the regime of communist

Socialism. [3]

This problem of democracy is crucial in the proletarian revolution. Democracy becomes the last bulwark of defense of Capitalism, an instrument used by dominant Capitalism and the *petite bourgeoisie* in a last desperate defense of private property. Any compromise on the issue of democracy compromises the integrity of the Revolution, stultifies its purposes and palsies its action: it is an issue pregnant with the potentiality of fatal mistakes. And yet it is all simplicity itself: in the revolution, the proletariat may depend upon itself alone; it alone is necessary in the process of production; it alone is a revolutionary class, implacably arrayed against all other classes; it alone counts as a class in the reconstruction of society, – and, accordingly, the dictatorship of the proletariat refuses political "rights" and recognition to any section of the bourgeois class.

Through its dictatorship, the proletariat, organizes itself as the ruling class, acquires social supremacy. The basis of the new "state" is not territorial, but industrial: its constituents are the organized producers. The other elements of the people function in this proletarian government in the meqsure that they are absorbed in the new industrial scheme of things, become useful producers. The process of transformation into communist socialism is a process of the organized producers, and of these alone. [4]

The dictatorship of the proletariat, naturally, will have many acute problems press upon it. Civil war, a revolutionary war, problems of general social reconstruction, – all these are problems that will call forth all of the energy, clarity and capacity of the proletarian revolution. The central problem, of course, is the problem of economic reconstruction. The particular initial form that this reconstruction assumes will depend upon a number of factors, particularly the factor of the degree of industrial development. In the **Communist Manifesto**, Marx and Engels said:

"The proletariat will use its political supremacy to wrest,

by degrees, all capital from the bourgeoisie; to centralize all instruments of production in the hands of the state – that is, of the proletariat organized as the ruling class; and to increase the total of productive forces as rapidly as possible. Of course, in the beginning this cannot be effected except by means of despotic inroads on the rights of property and on the conditions of bourgeois production; by measures, therefore, which appear economically insufficient and untenable, but which in the course of the movement, outstrip themselves, necessitate further inroads upon the old social order and are unavoidable as a means of entirely revolutionizing the mode of production."

The proletariat, in short, lays a dictatorial hand upon production. The control of industry is centralized in the administrative norms of the new proletarian state.

The dictatorship of the proletariat does not, necessarily, dispose all at once of the capitalist; what it does dispose of immediately are the *prerogatives* of the capitalist *as a capitalist*. The society of communist Socialism does not come into being as Minerva out of the head of Jove: it is a process of transformation of the old into the new. The rapidity of this transformation depends on the degree of economic development, and the rapidity with which the organized producers develop their own administrators. In a concentrated industry, where the process of production is managed by the technical staff and administrators, the capitalist is abolished at once; where not, the capitalist is retained and impressed into service as an expert and administrator, temporarily, until the whole process works itself out in complete industrial communism. Proletarian control is transformed into proletarian administration in all its phases, as the necessary maturity and institutions are developed.

The old relations of capitalist production are not torn asunder as one tears up a scrap of paper. The process is one of adaptation of means to purposes and of purposes to means. This may appear as the argument of petty bourgeois Socialism; but

186

there is all the difference in the world whether the process proceeds on the basis of bourgeois private property and under control of the bourgeois state, or whether it proceeds on the basis of proletarian control and a state of the dictatorship of the proletariat. The one promotes Capitalism and is a negation of Socialism, the other promotes Socialism and is a negation of Capitalism.

The proletariat's dictatorial control of production develops, on the one hand, the forces of production; and, on the other, it develops the communist administration of the industrial process. At first, the administration of control functions through general organizations, Councils of Workers. These organizations are gradually integrated, adapted to industrial divisions; and it is precisely at this point that industrial unionism, whether actual or potential, functions in the construction of the new society. Industry as a whole is divisible into constituent units, – the production of coal, of steel, of textiles, agriculture, transportation, etc. Each industry will constitute a department of the industrial state; the workers in each industry will organize in Local Councils and these unite into General Industrial Councils coordinated with other General Industrial Councils into a central administration of the whole productive process. Industrial unionism, organizing the producers industrially, becomes the vital basis of the new communist society, together with other administrative norms necessary to co-ordinate the non-industrial activity of society.

The industrial administration of communist Socialism institutes all the centralization necessary and compatible with autonomy, and all the autonomy necessary and compatible with centralization. The central administration is directive, and not repressive; it co-ordinates the whole industrial process as the General Industrial Council co-ordinates each phase of its particular industry; its functions are comprised in the statistical regulation and directive control of the forces of production.

The division of the product is ultimately determined on a

communistic basis: from each according to his ability, to each according to his needs.

The dictatorship of the proletariat is temporary, its necessity ceasing as the task of destroying the old order and organizing the new is accomplished. The rapidity of this development depends upon the maturity of proletarian consciousness and class power, upon the relation of social forces within the nation and upon the general international situation. The development of the proletarian revolution lets loose violent antagonisms within the nation, and the vitality of these antagonisms will affect the rapidity of development; the proletarian revolution, moreover, lets loose equally violent international antagonisms. As the revolutionary proletariat reconstructs society, it may find itself compelled simultaneously to wage civil wars and revolutionary wars. It may even, temporarily, meet defeat: the process consists of a series of revolutionary struggles. But the proletarian revolution, acting through the dictatorship of the proletariat, actual or potential, partial or complete, adhering firmly to the class struggle and revolutionary Socialism, is determined in a course of action against which nothing but betrayals can prevail.

Footnotes

1. Let there be no fatalism in our councils. The Socialist Republic is no predestined inevitable development ... The Socialist Republic will not leap into existence out of the existing social loom, like a yard of calico is turned out by a Northrop loom. Nor will its only possible architect, the Working Class – that is, the wage earner, or wage slave, the modern proletariat – figure in the process as a mechanical force moved mechanically. In other words, the world's theatre of Social Evolution is not a Punch and Judy box, nor are the actors on that world's stage mannikins, operated with wires ... The Socialist Republic depends, not upon material conditions only; it depends upon these – plus clearness of vision to assist the evolutionary process ... Is the revolutionary class of this Age living under ripened conditions to avail itself of its opportunity and fulfill its historic mission? Or is the

revolutionary spark of our Age to be smothered and banked up till, as in Rome of old, it leap from the furnace, a weapon of national suicide? In sight of the invasion of the Philippine Islands and the horrors that are coming to light, is there any to deny that the question is a burning one? – Daniel De Leon, **Two Pages From Roman History**, 1902.

2. As to the revolutionary organization and its task, the conquest of the power of the state and militarism: From the praxis of the Paris Commune, Marx shows that "the working class cannot simply lay hold of the ready-made machinery of the state, and wield it for its own purposes." The proletariat must break down this machinery. And this has been either concealed or denied by the opportunists. But it is the most valuable lesson of the Paris Commune and of the Revolution in Russia of 1905. The difference between us and the anarchists is, that we admit the state is a necessity in the development of our Revolution. The difference with the opportunists and the Kautsky disciples is that we claim we do not need the bourgeois state machinery as completed in the "democratic" bourgeois republics, but the direct power of armed and organized workers. Such is the state we need. Such was the character of the Commune of 1871 and of the Council of Workmen and Soldiers of 1905 and 1917. On this basis we build. – N. Lenin, *The Russian Revolution*, **The New International**, June 30, 1917.

3. During the course of events in Russia, democracy was a fetter upon the development of the proletarian revolution; once this revolution was accomplished, democracy became a counter-revolutionary instrument used by the petty bourgeois Socialism of the Mensheviki and Social-Revolutionists of the Right through the Constituent Assembly. If the Soviet government had not dissolved the Constituent Assembly, it would have stultified itself and the Revolution. The Revolution, declared the decree of dissolution, created the Workers' and Soldiers' Council – the only organization able to direct the struggle of the exploited classes for complete political and economic liberation; this Council constituted a revolutionary government through the November Revolution, after perceiving the illusion of an understanding with the bourgeoisie and its deceptive parliamentary organization; the Constituent Assembly, being elected from the old election lists, was the expression of the old regime when authority belonged to the bourgeoise, and necessarily became the authority of

the bourgeois republic, setting itself against the revolution of November and the authority of the Councils; the old bourgeois parliamentarism has had its day and is incompatible with the tasks before Socialism, and that only such institutions as the Workmen's and Soldiers' Councils are able to overcome the opposition of the ruling classes and create a new Socialist state; "the central executive committee, therefore, orders the Constituent Assembly dissolved."

4. "The economic activity of the modern state," says Karl Kautsky in **The Erfurt Program**, "is the natural starting point of the development that leads to the Co-operative Commonwealth." On the contrary; the natural starting point is the economic activity of the producers functioning industrially as an organized system.

Supplementary

I
Imperialism in Action

By Louis C. Fraina; reprinted from **The Class Struggle**, *September-October, 1918.*

THE institution of the Federal Reserve System during the first administration of Woodrow Wilson was an important development in the amalgamation of Capitalism and Imperialism. It realized, if not wholly, at least sufficiently for all purposes, the dream of finance-capital for a central bank. The older dream had been a central bank completely dominated by Big Capital, an expression of the epoch when a few financial magnates maintained supremacy, often to the injury of Capitalism as a whole. But with the amalgamation of Capitalism and Imperialism into State Capitalism, with the disappearance of America's splendid isolation, and the recognition of the necessity of a united capitalist class in the struggles of Imperialism and to secure world power, the older conception of a central bank had to be modified. It could no longer be simply an instrument of Big Capital; dominantly and necessarily an instrument of finance-capital, the central bank under the new conditions had to make ample provisions for the lesser groups and interests of Capitalism, become the instrument of a larger Capitalism. The Federal Reserve System met these requirements adequately. It unified the banking system of the country, solved minor antagonisms and amalgamated Capitalism, and freed finance capital for the struggle to secure the financial supremacy of the world.

The war offered a splendid opportunity for financial supremacy, and the Federal Reserve System, centralized in the Federal Reserve Board, responded successfully to the opportunity. Upon his resignation on August 9 as a member of the Federal Reserve Board, Paul M. Warburg, an active factor in the organization and operation of the Federal Reserve System, summarized its achievements in one sentence: "Nothing but mismanagement could wrest the financial premiership of the world from us." American Capitalism has definitely emerged into the epoch of international Imperialism.

The financial supremacy of the United States in world affairs is a direct consequence of its developing Imperialism. The centralization of the banking system, itself an expression of the amalgamation of Capitalism and Imperialism in State Capitalism, was a decisive instrument of action, the war accelerating the process by means of an unusual opportunity. Mr. Warburg, in an interview in the **New York Times** of August 18, pictures the process in excellent terms. Speaking of the form of the Federal Reserve System, he says:

"From a technical and banking standpoint, it might have been a better system to have one central bank with branches. Centralization is always an economy of power, and makes for greater efficiency. For political and other reasons it was essential to have the system as it is, and the proof of its wisdom lies in its success. With political, economic and social conditions what they are, a central bank would be likely to become the target of constant political attacks. There would always be suspicion of too extended a concentration of control either by capital or 'politics.' The present form offers a better protection in this regard, and the present system ought therefore to be better protected and to have better chance for untrammeled development than a full-fledged central bank."

The "political, economic and social conditions" mean the epoch of Imperialism, wherein finance-capital becomes the instrument of the whole of Capitalism, and not simply of a few dominant groups; wherein the process of expropriation takes a new form, being no longer dominantly the expropriation of one capitalist by another capitalist within the nation, but the expropriation of one national Capitalism by another; and the unifying of the national forces of Capitalism for the struggle to acquire world-power. Describing the achievements of the Federal Reserve System, Mr. Warburg says:

"We have brought into effective co-ordination a large portion of the country's banking reserves. We have regulated and brought about a general understanding of modern methods of re-discounting. We have created a world-wide market for bankers' acceptances, so that American trade is now largely financed by our own acceptances instead of by foreign ones, and at the same time our member banks now have an easy means of recourse to the Federal Reserve banks in case they wish to replenish their reserves.

"We have established fiscal agency relations with the Government and perfected an instrument which has proved of the greatest value in placing our issues of Government securities ... I believe I may say the world marvels at the ease with which we are constantly transferring hundreds of millions of dollars without creating any disturbance. Without the Federal Reserve machinery of clearing through the gold clearing fund and without the redeposit organization developed by them, acting as agents for the Government, that would have been entirely impossible.

"The Federal Reserve clearings per day amount now to over $400,000,000. For the first time in our history American banks have gone into foreign countries and opened branches – in Asia, Central and South America – as adjuncts to our growing trade."

Mr. Warburg realizes that these problems of finance are not simply problems of the banks, but of the whole of Capitalism. He realizes, moreover, the tendency toward the amalgamation of Capitalism and Imperialism into State Capitalism:

"In Europe after the war, the most efficient Government

promotion of industries in many lines will be held to exist in actual Government ownership and operation. More than ever will states become solid industrial and financial unions effectively organized for world competition, driven by the necessity of perfecting a system of the greatest efficiency, economy and thrift in order to be able to meet the incredible burdens created by the war.

"In this world of the future we shall have to maintain our own position, and it requires on our part thorough organization and steady leadership. Under our democratic system this cannot be furnished by changing party governments, but can only be provided by fairly permanent, non-partisan and expert bodies. These bodies must combine the judicial point of view with that of active and constructive business minds. They must be able to act as expert advisers to Congress and to the industries concerned. They must break down the suspicion and prejudice of Government against business and business against Government. They must stand for the interest of all against the exaction or aggression of any single individual or group, be it called labor or capital, carrier or shipper, lender or borrower, Republican or Democrat.

"Our ability to handle effectually the great economic problems of the future will depend upon developing boards and commissions of sufficient expert knowledge and independence of character. This will be possible only if both Government and people fully appreciate the importance of such bodies, so that the country may find its ablest sons willing to render public service worthy of the personal sacrifice it entails ...

"It appears inevitable that America will be one of the dominating financial powers in the coming era of peace. Indeed, if we play our cards right and if the war ends within a reasonable time, we should be the dominating financial power of the world. When peace comes we should command the three essentials that would assure us an unassailable strategic commercial position – the raw materials, the ships and the gold.

"The world at large is indebted to us. Nothing but mismanagement could wrest the financial premiership of the world from us."

This is an excellent description, by a dominant actor on the stage of finance-capital, of the characteristics of Imperialism. "More than ever will states become solid industrial and financial unions effectively organized for world competition"; boards of experts are to become the real governing factor in State Capitalism, since the problems are complex and technical, and continuity of policy, (which the laggard bourgeoisie of Finland wish to secure by means of a Prussianized monarchy), is indispensable to Imperialism; "organization and steady leadership" are prime requirements, and "under our democratic system this cannot be furnished by changing party governments." This is precisely the important characteristic of Imperialism, – the reaction against democracy and the parliamentary system. "Changing party governments" are fundamental to bourgeois democracy and the parliamentary system; the abrogation of their function, by centralizing actual power in an administrative dictatorship and administrative boards, means the end of the parliamentary regime. Imperialism requires a unified Capitalism, a centralized banking system acting through finance-capital, and a centralized administrative control, parliaments being degraded to an "advisory" capacity.

The acquisition by American Capitalism of "the financial premiership of the world" necessarily means a transformation of its foreign policy. The indications of this transformation have been many, and are multiplying.

In 1913, the Administration declined to support American participation in the Six-Power Loan to China, President Wilson declaring that the terms of the loan "touch very nearly the administrative independence of China." At the time this action was considered a fundamental departure from accepted policy in foreign affairs, and the initiation of a democratic era in international diplomacy. But in July of this year the government approved the proposed loan of $50,000,000 to China by an American financial group, agreeing "to make prompt and vigorous representations and to take every possible step" to insure China's fulfilling its financial obligations. Moreover, the bankers are throughout to be guided by "the policies outlined by the Department of State." This is a unity of government and finance-capital characteristic of Imperialism.

The Six-Power Loan was to be secured by China's pledge of the salt tax, an internal levy, as security; its administration was to be reorganized under foreign auspices, and if this proved unsatisfactory, representatives of the powers making the loan might assume entire control of the tax – terms which, in the words of President Wilson, "touch very nearly the adminstrative independence of China." But this was not the crux of the issue; the decisive feature was the political character of the loan, the governments of the bankers becoming its guarantors. The new American loan to China is based on no security at all, and in that it differs from the Six-Power Loan; but is identical in its political character, the American government becoming its guarantor. This is a political transaction; and political loans have been a fruitful source of international antagonisms. In these financial tranactions of Imperialism, a government pledges all the resources of diplomacy, and as a final resort its military might, to assure the security of loans and investments in undeveloped nations.

This transformation in foreign policy is in accord with the new position of the United States as a financial world power, and is latent with dangerous international complications.

Recent negotiations with Mexico are another indication of the policy of Imperialism. The Mexican government's most difficult problem is to limit the power of foreign capital, which secured a strangle hold upon the country's resources (and politics) through the concessions of the Diaz regime. The new constitution, accordingly, declares that "all contracts and concessions made by the former government from and after 1876, which shall have resulted in the monopoly of land, waters and natural resources of the nation by a single individual or corporation, are declared subject to revision, and the executive is authorized to declare those null and void which seriously prejudice the public interest." Ownership in lands or waters may be acquired only by Mexicans "by birth or naturalization," and in Mexican companies subject to the sovereign authority and laws of Mexico; ownership may be acquired by foreigners "provided they agree before the department of foreign affairs to be considered Mexicans in respect to such property, and accordingly not to invoke the protection of their government in respect to the same, under penalty, in case of breach, of forfeiture to the nation of property so acquired." All this is simply the assertion of the sovereignty inherent in a nation, and indisputably recognized by the law of nations. The problem of foreign capital is a crucial problem in Mexico, the prevailing conditions making it practically an appanage of international Imperialism. The raw materials and natural wealth of Mexico are to become factors in the promotion of Mexican Capitalism and national supremacy, not the means of exploitation of international finance-capital and Imperialism – this is the policy of the new Mexico.

Early this year the Mexican government promulgated a law imposing a heavy tax upon the development of oil, a very important industry, the foreign owners of which having been one of the most reactionary and brutal factors under the Diaz regime, and counter-revolutionary. American and British interests have more than $300,000,000 invested in the oil production of Mexico, and they unanimously declared that the new tax was confiscatory. They appealed to Ambassador Fletcher, who discussed their grievances with the American department of state. In April, Ambassador Fletcher transmitted a note to the Mexican government, declaring the tax law to be "confiscatory," that it was "taking property without due process of law," and that "it became the function of the government of the United States most earnestly and respectfully to call the attention of the Mexican government to the necessity which may arise to impel it to protect the property of its citizens in Mexico divested or injuriously affected by the decree above cited. If Mexico insists upon the execution of the law, there can be only one result."

This interference in the sovereign affairs of a nation is in accord with the finest traditions of imperialistic diplomacy. The power to tax is supreme, and cannot be abridged by any foreign power except through conquest. According to the Constitution of Mexico, the fundamental law of the land, the government has the power to impose this tax; if foreign investors consider the tax illegal, they should have recourse to the Mexican courts for redress, if any. That is the procedure in all strong and independent nations. Instead, these investors adopt the imperialistic means of asking their government to bring political pressure to bear upon the Mexican government – to violate its own constitution, and act as if it was the fundamental law only when it wasn't abrogated by the power of a foreign government.

This attitude of the investors was emphasized by an interview recently in the **New York Times**, in which a representative of oil interests in Mexico brazenly and unashamed proposed a conspiracy to compel the American and British governments to intervene in Mexico. This was the plan of the conspiracy: the Allied navies require a vast amount of oil, and most of it now comes from Mexico; if the Mexican government insists upon imposing the tax, the foreign oil interests will cease production, the Allied navies will be irreparably injured; and the Allied governments will be compelled, as a war measure, to intervene in Mexico. The tactics of highwaymen are mild in comparison with this proposed conspiracy. These investors are out to secure rights not accorded Mexican citizens, to acquire a privileged status above the law, and to use the military might of their governments as an instrument to promote their rapacious plans of plunder.
Using governments as instruments of finance-capital is

198

an essential procedure of Imperialism. Accepted as a policy, it becomes an implacable producer of antagonisms latent with the threat of war.

Imperialism necessarily abrogates the sovereignty of a nation upon which it would prey. The Lansing-Ishii Agreement concluded between the United States and Japan last year, is of a character to impair the sovereignty of China. The heart of the Agreement is this: "The Governments of the United States and Japan recognize that territorial propinquity creates special relations between countries, and, consequently, the Government of the United States recognizes that Japan has special interests in China, particularly in the part to which her possessions are contiguous." The Chinese government, very rightly, complained of an agreement concerning China about which China was not consulted, and declared it would not recognize the Agreement. Special rights based upon "territorial propinquity" – this is a policy of Imperialism. True enough, the Agreement declares: "The Governments of the United States and Japan deny that they have any purpose to infringe in any way on the independence or territorial integrity of China." But since Japan voluntarily accepted the policy of the "open door," formulated by John Hay, Japan has fought an imperialistic war against Russia concerning control of Chinese territory, and closed the doors, and double-bolted them, in Eastern Inner Mongolia, South Manchuria, Fukien, Shantung, and lesser places. The whole of Capitalism is now in the orbit of Imperialism. Imperialism molds the destiny of the nations. In the days to come, Imperialism will determine all things and rend the world in the savagery of its struggle – unless revolutionary Socialism directs the hosts of the proletariat to the conquest of Capitalism and Imperialism.

Supplementary

II
Concentration and Labor

[This article by Louis C. Fraina appeared in **The International Socialist Review** of August, 1913, under the title *The Call of the Steel Worker*. It is reprinted whereas supplementary to the analysis of concentration, as a general tendency, made in earlier chapters of this book, and to illustrate the specific effects of concentration on wages and conditions of labor.

[The steel industry is typical of concentrated industry and of Imperialism, the nerve-center of modern capitalist production. It is an industry that constitutes the material factor in waging war today; and it profits most from war and Imperialism.

[This article describes the *normal* conditions of the steel industry, not its abnormal war aspects. Obviously, under war conditions, the degree of exploitation and of profits are each increased. A light is thrown upon these conditions by the report of John A. Topping, chairman of the Board of Directors of the Republic Iron and Steel Company, made at the annual stockholders' meeting on April 17, 1918. Mr. Topping reported total profits for the year 1917 of $38,769,021.39, and said: "*The Republic Iron and Steel Company can be said to have been reborn and remade.*" The profits of the United States Steel Corporation have been phenomenal.

[The steel industry is an animating factor in Imperialism; the steel workers will yet become an animating factor in the proletarian revolution.]

"I never had a strike as long as I was in the steel business." Andrew Carnegie, Angel of Peace with the heart of steel, made that astounding statement to the Stanley Steel Investigating Committee. Expansively, benignantly, Andrew of the gentle soul and cultural urge gave his lying testimony – under oath. Homestead? Braddocks?

The lie was too much for the committee. It was such a crass, palpable, stupid lie. Carnegie was compelled to retract and admit strikes. But having saved its neck, the committee wished to go no further and decided that the bloody annals of Homestead were "really extraneous to the investigation."

"Let's not open up the old sores," pleaded Congressman Gardner, Republican.

"I agree with Mr. Gardner that it would be unkind to Mr. Carnegie," acquiesced Stanley, Democrat.

"Unkind"? Men slain in cold blood to insure profits; unionism crushed. Where at Homestead there was one plate mill in 1892 employing three crews of men working eight hours a day, now there are four mills each with *two* crews, *working twelve hours a day*; work increased 50 per cent and wages only 20 per cent. "Unkind"? It is "unkind" to remind the perpetrator of this of his villainy; but it is not "unkind" for such degrading conditions to exist. Blessed be Capital in its Holiness!

This typical piece of capitalist hypocrisy has since been put into the shade. As with machinery, capitalist hypocrisy of yesteryear is always being improved upon – progress in all things! Testifying for the defense in the suit to dissolve the United States Steel Corporation, former Ambassador Bacon said that "love of his fellow-men," of the workers (!?!), was the basic motive that led J. Pierpont Morgan to organize the steel trust. "His first great object," testified Mr. Bacon, "was by reason of the decrease in the cost of production to make it

202

possible to improve the conditions of labor by increasing wages and bettering conditions." Amplifying this, the **New York Commercial**, June 18, 1913, said with editorial effrontery:

"The new regime of iron and steel production has been singularly free from this bellicose attitude on the part of labor. It may be attributed in a large measure to the Morgan idea that to get the best results of heavily capitalized industry, it must be organized on a basis which permits a large and generous study of the interests of labor."

Amen!

And, of course, if we accept the statements in the "Amen!" spirit, and that is the purpose, the Press now playing the *role* of Church, they are gospel truth. But being Infidels, we investigate:

- Since the formation of the Steel Trust in 1902 profits have proven huge and inexhaustible.
- Simultaneously, *total wages have been reduced*, and individual wages only *slightly* increased. *Comparing this slight increase with higher prices, actual wages have been heavily reduced.*
- From 1902 to the quarter ended March 31, 1913, Steel Trust profits total $1,397,383,092. With the exception of 1904 and 1908, yearly profits have always exceeded the hundred-million mark – 166 odd millions in 1902, 160-odd millions in 1907, etc. The lowest profit was in 1904, being 73-odd millions. And these profits are even huger than the figures show, for by over capitalization, financial jugglery and a misleading system of accounts, profits are systematically underestimated.

Obviously, the Steel Trust has been a bonanza to its owners. Heavily-capitalized industry pays. But this "prosperity" is a sort of mirage in the desert to the proletariat.

Examining the figures compiled by the Bureau of Labor report for the pig iron branch of the Steel Trust, we ascertain:

1. In Pennsylvania mills in 1902 the Trust employed 37,191 men, who produced 8,111,000 tons of pig iron.
2. In 1909, the workers had *decreased* numerically to 14,921; yet their output *increased* 2,610,024 tons – they produced 10,721,024 tons of pig iron. And the men were employed fewer days.
3. Total wages in 1902, $10,191,579; in 1909, $7,702,304 – *a decrease in wages* of $2,489,275.
4. The average daily wage in seven years increased *twenty cents*.
5. Output per man increased from 1.51 to 2.39 tons in the seven years. Labor-cost per ton decreased from $1.25 to $0.82 per ton.

The facts of pig iron apply to the steel industry as a whole, and to concentrated Capitalism.

Concentrated capital, the form to which all capital trends, means greater power of exploitation. Concentrated capital means:

1. Availing itself of the most efficient existing machinery, and improving that machinery, concentrated capital extracts an increasingly large volume of surplus value from the proletariat.
2. Simultaneously with greater output flowing from machinery, productivity of labor is increased by the *form* of work – large co-operative activity, "the collective power of masses."
3. This increased productivity proceeds simultaneously with relatively *lesser* number of employees; hence increasing unemployment and competition, thereby preventing a general rise in wages.
4. While marshaling the workers into an industrial army, concentrated capital succeeds in destroying the potential proletarian power of this army by dividing the workers with a variety of schemes.
5. The workers only gradually awaken to a sense of the

power which is their's by being organized in the "labor army" of concentrated capital; but the awakening comes, sooner or later.

6. In the meantime, concentrated capital sweats out of the proletariat fabulous profits, while actually paying less wages, and, socially measured, making worse the condition of the proletariat.

The Bureau of Labor recently made public a special report of its investigation into the iron and steel industry as a whole. The investigation covers the period of May, 1910, embracing 212 blast furnaces and steel plants, employing 172,706 men.

Of the total 172,706 employees, 13,868, or 8.03 per cent, received less than 14 cents per hour; 20,527, or 11.89 per cent, received 14 and under 16 cents; and 51,417, or 29.77 per cent, received 16 and under 18 cents. Thus 85,812, or 49.69 per cent of all employees, received less than 18 cents per hour.

Those receiving 18 and under 25 cents per hour numbered 46,132, or 26.71 per cent; while 40,762, or 23.61 per cent, earned 25 cents and over. A few very highly skilled employees received $1.25 per hour; and those receiving 50 cents and over per hour numbered 4,403, or 2.55 per cent of all employees.

Figuring on a 12-hour day, 131,944 employees, or 76.4 per cent of the total, received from $1.68 to $3.00 in daily wages, while half of the men received from $1.68 to $2.16.

On February 1, 1913, the Steel Trust made "a general increase in wages and salaries, averaging for employees receiving less than $2 per day about 12½ per cent." We do not know whether the increase has actually been made; we must take Chairman Gary's word for it. But if it has the "increase" is a mere bagatelle compared with the gigantic rise in the cost of living and the yield of profits.

It must be observed that despite this "increase" in wages,

which Gary claims is $12,000,000, profits of the Steel Corporation for the first quarter of 1913 were higher from eight to twenty million dollars for eight years, and lower from five to two millions for three years. So huge is labor's yield of surplus value in trustified industry that profits are always large despite "increased operating expenses."

The picture drawn by steel mill wages is one of grinding, agonizing toil, of a machine existence – just enough oil in the form of wages to keep the human machine going. The $1.68 to $2.16 daily wage is even lower, considering that few steel workers are steadily employed. Social workers estimate that $700 to $800 is the minimum yearly income to sustain a proletarian family on *common necessaries*. Most of these steel workers never earn that. They must, therefore, live a materially sub-human existence.

Not only are wages low, but hours of work are extraordinarily high, Of the 172,706 steel workers investigated by the Bureau of Labor, 50,000 or 29 per cent, customarily toiled seven days per week, and 20 per cent sweated 84 hours or more per week, which means a 12-hour working day every blessed day in the week, including Sunday. Nearly 43 per cent of the men were found working 72 hours per week, or 12 hours per day for a 6-day week. Men often toil 20 to 30 hours at a stretch. A plan is mooted to give the 7-day men one day off a week, but this would not affect the 72-hour a week men. Toil would continue frightful.

The hypocritical plea of the steel barons is that a "metallurgical necessity" exists for the 7-day week, for continuous operation. But this continuous operation could be secured without sweating the men seven days a week. The plea is a dastardly subterfuge. The investigators developed the fact that the 7-day week was not confined to the blast furnace department, where there is a "metallurgical necessity" for continuous operation, and where 88 per cent of the men toil seven days a week; but it was found that, to a considerable

206

extent, in other departments where no "metallurgical necessity" exists, work was also carried on Sundays.

In an effort to silence public opposition the Steel Corporation made a bluff to remedy these horrible conditions. A committee of stockholders was appointed to investigate the 12-hour day, which said among other things:

"We are of the opinion that a 12-hour day of labor, followed continuously by any group of men for any considerable number of years, *means a decreasing of the efficiency* and lessening of the vigor and virility of such men." (My italics)

The Finance Committee than appointed a sub-committee which reported against the change at the stockholders' meeting of April 21, 1913, on the ground that "unless competing iron and steel manufacturers will also enforce a less than 12-hour day, the effort to reduce the twelve hours per day at all our works will result in losing a large number of our employees, many of them preferring to take positions requiring more hours of work per day."

A mesh of hypocritical pretense. The matter of competition cuts no figure, for the "trust" has "gentle men's agreements" with the "independents" not only concerning prices, but conditions of labor. They are agreed to crush labor, but *do not wish* to agree to "improve" labor. Another subterfuge John A. Fitch exposes in the **Survey**:

"Of course, nothing is said in this report, nor was anything said at the stockholders' meeting, as to the real reason why workers leave their positions.

"The facts are that the cost of this reform was borne by the men. The Steel Corporation did not pay its men their old earnings for their new six-day stint."

Economic necessity, and not that "the men like to work twelve hours a day," as Judge Gary impudently claims, compels these men to toil inhumanly.

207

Nevertheless, an 8-hour day in the steel mills is only a matter of time. Capitalists are recognizing that non-sweated labor is the most efficient. This reform, says the **Boston Transcript**, "experts declare will increase, rather than diminish, dividends." And the Bureau of Labor argues that –

From the experience of English blast-furnace owners who have adopted the eight-hour shift system, and from the experience in other industries, it will tend to produce a much more efficient force of workmen. There is no increase in "cost of production," and the quality of the product improves greatly.

The steel barons have a purely capitalist interest in their slaves, not at all human. Recently, steel superintendents in certain Pennsylvania steel towns appeared in court and argued against granting saloons licenses, *as saloons menaced their profits, drink sapping the workers' efficiency.*

Intoxication is a logical result of steady, grinding toil. And saloons flourish in steel towns. Toil in steel plants, especially in the blast furnaces, saps vitality and develops an overpowering desire for stimulants. The men drink, and drink, for in drink their sorrow vanishes any they have a momentary thrill of pleasure. And many, if not most, drink because of a blind, dumb, rooted resentment. They hate the boss, they hate work, they hate themselves, they hate life. This resentment and hatred shall be harnessed to the mighty ends of the Revolution.

It was during the Passaic, N.J., textile strike. I was interviewing one of the strikers, a wisp of a Polish girl of sixteen. Toil in the industrial Bastile had not yet dried the red of her cheeks.

"My mother lives in Pittsburgh," she said. "I send her what I can. My father worked in the steel mill, worked hard and long. Then he began to drink, and became unkind. Oh, yes, he was good before that. One day his arm was cut off and he became worse. Then mother and I had to leave him."

"Do you ever see your father now?"

"Never. And we don't want to, either. But I saw very little of him in the old days, he worked so long."

The Steel Trust plumes itself on having had no strikes. "There have been no strikes or disturbances in the operation of the great steel company, and comparatively few in its more powerful rivals, which have patterned after its ideals and labor plans," says the **Commercial**. The reason thereof is plain. The Steel Trust terrorizes its employees and holds them in mental, physical and spiritual bondage – for the Church in the steel centers is owned body and soul by the exploiters. The men are forbidden to organize. They must present grievances individually; even a committee must not be formed. A comprehensive spy system is maintained; men are afraid to talk for fear of discharge. An investigator says:

"I called one day at the home of a skilled steel worker, an employee of the United States Steel Corporation, and he sent his wife to the door to tell me that he couldn't talk with me because the company had 'given orders that the men shouldn't talk about mill work.' There was a wage cut at Homestead in 1908 that set the whole town talking around their firesides. But on the street the men would deny all knowledge of it."

The associative spirit is crushed. The workers dare not act collectively; the trust takes care that they don't; and individually they are helpless. Any move collectively to improve conditions means discharge. In 1906 the workers of Jones & Laughlin, powerful "independents," planned a meeting of protest against Sunday work. The superintendent threatened with discharge whoever attended the meeting. *The meeting was not held.* This practice is general in the iron and steel industry.

Then there is the "pension system." Pensions rivet employees to the employer. They are a chain-ball on the ankle of proletarian action.

The steel industry has applied the "efficiency system" with marked success. One phase of the "efficiency system" is the more intensive exploitation of the human unit in production; the other phase, more important to the capitalist at the present stage of things, is holding the worker in subjection and discouraging union organization.

Work, Wages and Profits by H.L. Gantt, a book written for employers and published by **The Engineering Magazine**, New York, gives the snap away. Gantt advocates the "efficient utilization of labor"; this implies getting the worker to increase his output, and as one of the means of doing this the "task and bonus" system is offered. The work is divided into "tasks" and apportioned among the workers. The man who completes his task within the time set by the superintendent (time being decided by the most rapid worker) receives a "bonus." Instituted in the plants of the Bethlehem Steel Company, the assistant superintendent after two months' trial wrote that the method had *"eliminated the constant necessity for driving the men."* Gantt says that "the average monthly output of the shop from March 1, 1900, to March 1, 1901, was 1,173,000 pounds, and from March 1, 1901, to August 1, 1901 (after the 'bonus' system was inaugurated), it was 2,069,000 pounds." *The shop employed 700 men and paid on the "bonus" plan only 80 workers out of the entire 700.*

The "task and bonus" scheme decreases "cost of production" and increases the workers' yield of surplus value at small additional expense to the employer, as only a *few* receive the "bonus." It eliminates the "necessity for driving," as the worker, lured on by the "bonus" will-o-wisp, becomes his own slave-driver.

"So far this system has never failed to create a strong spirit of harmony and co-operation" between employer and employees; it shatters union efforts, as the employer uses the scheme to separate the "bonus" receivers from the unsuccessful ones, creating a sort of "bonus aristocracy." Gantt opposes labor unions and employers' associations as they can never "effect a permanent solution of the problem of the proper relations between employers and employees"; his "task and bonus" system does bring about "proper relations," as it *discourages labor unions by inciting workers to strive individually, instead of collectively, to increase their wages.* What Marx, in **Capital**, said of wages, applies to the "efficiency" movement – "The rise of wages, therefore, is confined within limits that not only leave intact the foundations of the capitalistic system, but also secure its reproduction on a progressive scale."

But capitalist chicane cannot stifle the revolutionary spirit. The very effort to stifle creates the revolutionary spirit. There is a revolutionary group, a small group, but that matters not, among the steel workers. And they are biding their time. Revolt is near. It is bound to come. It is here. John A. Fitch recites a typical episode:

"It was a family of intelligence and breeding, and evidently of strong religious principles. The father had been telling me about the experience in a long life as a workman. The son had sat silently acquiescent in his father's analysis of existing conditions, but following the conversation with attention. Finally, addressing both, I asked what, in their judgment, would be the outcome of the unrest and discontent? There was silence for a moment and then the father shook his head sadly and said: 'There is no way out. There will be no change.' But the son cried out through set teeth: 'Yes, there is a way out, and it is through an armed revolution.'"

Steel conditions are universal, the steel industry being typical of trustified Capitalism. Trust-Capitalism creates a new proletariat, the proletariat of machine-tenders, of common, unskilled labor. Says the Bureau of Labor report: "Large as is the proportion that unskilled labor forms of the total labor force in the iron and steel industry, steel experts have noted the fact that the tendency of recent years has been steadily toward the reduction of the number of highly skilled men employed and *the establishment of the general wage on the basis of common or unskilled labor.*" (My italics.) Wages paid common labor in the steel industry are the wages of common labor everywhere. There is an identity in exploitation. This develops fraternal spirit, and, coupled with its strategic industrial position, makes common labor the revolutionary force.

Our agitation, our organization efforts must recognize this fact: *Common labor dominates industry.* And when common labor in steel revolts, when this basic industry feels the clutch of the Revolution, Capitalism will be shaken to its depths. The revolt of the steel workers will sound the call for the Social Revolution.